ON THE BACKS OF
BURROS

BRINGING CIVILIZATION TO COLORADO

BY P. DAVID SMITH
AND LYN BEZEK

WESTERN REFLECTIONS PUBLISHING COMPANY®

Lake City, CO

ISBN 978-1-932738-94-0

Library of Congress Control Number: 2010925527

Cover photo: "Chrysanthemum," The Burro Book,
Author's Collection
Cover and text design: Laurie Goralka Design

First Edition
Printed in the United States of America

Western Reflections Publishing Company®
P.O. Box 1149
951 N. Highway 149
Lake City, CO 81235
www.westernreflectionspublishing.com
(970) 944-0110

*Dedicated to the hundreds of thousands of burros
that did not have a good home*

Table of Contents

ॐ

Preface

ᗧ

Both *P. David Smith and Lyn Bezek* have had a long-time affection for the extraordinary beauty and amazing heritage of Colorado and the homely but precious little burro that consistently shows up in their home state's history. Through research and observation they have come to believe that the burro has given more to humanity and received less in return than any other creature throughout the history of Colorado, and perhaps the world.

The burro has been the friend and protector of the lonely Colorado prospector — patiently carrying his supplies, laboriously bringing heavy loads of ore to the smelters, and intently listening to his master's dreams and sorrows being related around the campfire. The burro has helped to defend the Colorado rancher's livestock from deadly predators yet has also been a loving, gentle companion to tens of thousands of women and children. With seemingly tireless determination, burros have transported millions of tons of supplies to isolated mining towns and mines, bringing civilization to the remote and rugged mountains of Colorado. However, in return, the burro has often been abused, ridiculed, grossly overworked, abandoned or even killed when its work was done. Only a few lucky animals were fed and taken care of, mainly by women and children who used them as pets or riding animals. The other burros either reverted back to their innate skills in the wild or they died.

Author P. David Smith has been interested in the mighty, little burro since he was seven years old, when his grandfather bought him and his brother a burro. "Prunes" had a corral made of aspen logs behind the house, and the boys could go back and saddle him up whenever they wanted. It was almost as good as getting a car a decade later. Prunes never bucked nor did anything that would hurt anyone; but Prunes did, unfortunately, start braying at his loudest at sunrise (about 5 A.M.). Neighbors (and especially the nearby tourist resort owners) did not appreciate the wake up call, so Prunes went back to his previous owner after only one summer.

As David later became interested in and started writing about Colorado history, he recognized the very special relationship that some pioneers, and in particular prospectors, had with their burros. It became especially evident in the large number of old Colorado photographs showing both rugged prospectors and little children hugging or even kissing the homely little

Author P. David Smith's mother on their burro "Prunes" near Crested Butte in 1952.
Author P. David Smith Collection

animals. Yet research also revealed that many burros were horribly mistreated or even killed, sometimes just for the fun of it.

David noticed that the books written by the pioneers of early-day Colorado almost always mentioned the burro. This long-eared animal was an important part of the state's local "color," as well as an important part of the Old West. Burros are present in thousands of early Colorado photographs, but they were not sleek, or slim, or fast. However they were an icon, much as the "Woodie" identified a surfer of the 1960s, or a Hummer showed the identity of an outdoors type in the 2000s.

Author Lyn Bezek was given the book *Brighty of the Grand Canyon*, written by famous author Marguerite Henry, when she was a little girl growing up in Pennsylvania Dutch farm country. There was something about the wonderful story of a little burro roaming free in the exotic canyons of the American West that completely captured her imagination. She can still

The classic tale of Brighty of the Grand Canyon *inspired author Lyn Bezek to write her own children's book about a donkey.*
Author Lyn Bezek Collection

remember Brighty's lovable face on the cover of her dog-eared copy of the book.

After college, Lyn headed west, eventually settling in Colorado, where she was thrilled to discover the "world famous" wild donkey herd in the historic town of Cripple Creek (they call the animal "donkey" in Cripple Creek," but "burro" in most of Colorado). Believed to be descendants of the prospector's donkeys that once toiled in the lucrative gold fields of the area, these animals are now the proud mascots of the town and wander free for much of the year. They serve as a symbol of a bygone era when burros were indispensible partners of humans in the building of Colorado and the West.

Whenever Lyn visits Cripple Creek — which since 1991 has been a gambling mecca — she tries to track down the local donkeys, and if she is successful she feels like she has really hit the jackpot. For her, card games and slot machines are not nearly as exciting as hanging out with the herd.

Just what is it about these sturdy little animals that draws her to them? Well, for starters, she loves their long floppy ears, their soulful eyes, and their surprisingly long eyelashes. She admires their long-suffering patience, their innate dignity, and their mysterious spiritual nature. She even gets a kick out of their ridiculous, ear-splitting brays, which always make her wonder if they are laughing at the foolishness of mankind.

The more Lyn learns about donkeys, the more she is captivated by them. Despite centuries of abuse, overwork, and ridicule, they have managed to forgive, adapt, and even thrive. They are true survivors. Lyn agrees with one writer who suggested their oversized ears enable them to "listen to the Universe." She is sure they have much donkey wisdom to share with all of us, if only we are clever enough to listen.

When **Lyn Bezek** wrote her children's book, *Daisy, the Cripple Creek Donkey,* she and her publisher, ***P. David Smith,*** had several long talks about the misconceptions and mistreatment of the burro in Colorado. Both agreed that burros deserved better, and that their true story needed to be told — not the tall tale of dumb, lazy, and stubborn animals, but rather the facts about a gentle, sweet, hard working, and very complex creature.

Although still not fully safe or appreciated, the burro seems to finally be on the trail to getting some of the respect and validation that it should get. Yet, many Americans do not know what a burro looks like, what its traits are, or what its history is. It is our hope that this book will help the burro further along the path to receiving the full recognition that it has earned by sweat, pain, and toil, and which it so justly deserves.

Acknowledgements

From P. David Smith:

There are always many people to thank when doing a book like this. I would like to give my special appreciation to these extra special people.

Thanks to Marty Priest for doing some of the book's interviews, helping with locating photographs and illustrations, and for her great editing skills.

To Coi Gehrig of the Denver Public Library Western History Department for very fast and efficient help in getting copies of the photos from the DPL Collection. I also think that the Denver Public Library does an excellent job of promoting and distributing the great history of our state.

To Beth Hurd for talking to us at length about her three precious miniature donkeys and what makes them so special.

To my wife Jan, who puts up with my spending hours on the computer and in my library, while I follow up on the other loves of my life — the history of Colorado and the Old West.

To Grant Houston, editor of Lake City's *Silver World*, who supplied the great story about Old Sid and other tidbits about Lake City's burros.

To many other friends who knew I was working on this book and gave me a photo, a clipping, or other little bits of history over the last five years.

From Lyn Bezek:
I would like to acknowledge and thank the many burro experts who so graciously and enthusiastically shared their knowledge and love of burros with me during the researching and writing of this book.

First, I am indebted to burro racers Curtis Imrie, Dave TenEyck, Bill Lee, Barb Dolan, Ralph Herzog, John Vincent, Brad Wann, and Hal Walter for all their valuable input. While interviewing these human athletes who take part in the incredible sport of burro racing, I discovered that they are very much like their burro running partners—smart, sociable, patient, humble, tolerant, generous, adaptable, dependable, strong, resilient, courageous, noble, and long-suffering. Three cheers for all the humans and burros who help keep Colorado's unique, indigenous sport alive year after year.

I am grateful to Tom and Judy Cooper, Melissa Trenary, Bill and Nancy Loop, and Jan Collins, who shared their stories about Cripple Creek's beloved wild donkey herd. Thank you to all the Two Mile High Club members and Cripple Creek citizens who protect and care for their long-eared town mascots.

My gratitude also goes to Fran Ackley, Wild Horse and Burro Specialist in Cañon City, for his hands-on perspective about the Bureau of Land Management program as well as for arranging my visit with Radar, the BLM's photogenic and charismatic burro ambassador. Thank you to Etta Windwalker and Shelley Riddock for introducing me to their wonderful donkeys and for being such loving and responsible pet owners.

An especially big thank you is deserved by Kathy Dean, Executive Director of Longhopes Donkey Shelter, whose passion, dedication, and expertise shine through in everything she does for Colorado's donkeys and donkeys everywhere. Kathy has been our "go to person" and an invaluable resource in the writing of this book.

I also would like to acknowledge and thank my talented technical support person and friend, Jan Pacheco, for her patience and computer guidance.

And, last but not least, I want to thank my generous and long-suffering husband, Mike, who willingly drives me all over the state of Colorado on my book-related missions. It's been a fun ride.

CHAPTER ONE

☪

A Donkey, a Burro, or an Ass?
The Lineage of the Burro

Although known by several other names, the small beast of burden with the big eyes, large head, and extra long ears, which is now generally known in Colorado as the "burro," has been with us for thousands of years. DNA testing dates the wild burro back to well over 10,000 years ago. The ancient Egyptians began to domesticate burros and include them in their drawings about 4,000 B. C., and the fuzzy, little animal has proven to be a good and faithful worker for mankind ever since. The burro is not native to the Americas, but rather arrived in the late fifteenth century with the domesticated European horse and mule.

There are today only five living animals in the biological genus *equus*, which includes the burro — three species of zebras, one of horses, and one of asses (which is a shortening of the scientific classification of *asinus*). The specie is *equus africanus asinus* and it has two subspecies — *asinus somaliensis* (Somalian Wild Ass) and *asinus africus* (Nubian Wild Ass). The burros that we see today in Colorado are descended from the wild *asinus africus*, which originated in northern Africa and, over time, spread around the Mediterranean Sea and eventually made its way into southern Europe about 2,000 B. C. Because of domestication, the wild ass in Africa has almost vanished. It is estimated that less than 600 *asinus africus* are left in the wild. However there is an initiative to formally recognize the approximately 5,000 wild burros in the United States as being part of *asinnus africus*. At any rate, the sub-species is nowhere close to being extinct, it is merely becoming domesticated. While the species of today's American burro is still *equus africanus asinus*, there is speculation that another species class may soon be formed for the domesticated ass.

The words "burro" and "ass" have been used for many centuries, yet the word "donkey" only developed into common usage in fairly recent times. Before the late 1700s the animal was always called an "ass" in the English language. The term "ass" started to fall out of use as a name for the animal in the late 1700s, with the word "donkey" coming into usage at basically the same time. The term "ass" was probably dropped because of the new, semi-vulgar use of that word to describe a human's posterior (technically the human backside is "arse," but this was changed with slang to "ass").

Burros were primarily used in ancient times for the transportation of goods, firewood, and water, but they were also sometimes used for riding. Since they are especially gentle animals, they were often chosen to be ridden by women and children. Most of the smaller members of the ass family were located in Spanish speaking countries and were called *"borricco,"* which it is believed was corrupted in English into "burro." The Spanish name for the burro probably came from the Latin name *"burrcus,"* which means "small horse." However, legend also has it that "burro" is a Spanish sound that is the equivalent to "gitty up" in English, which were words that were often used to keep the animal moving.

This sleepy little burro, shown in a photograph entitled "The Pioneer's Friend," has droopy ears that stick out instead of being in the usual "upright" position.
                    The Burro Book, Author's Collection

Although donkeys and burros are exactly the same animal genetically, it became popular in northern Europe to breed the larger asses to good-size mares to produce mules. Because of this practice, there are now, hundreds of years later, noticeable physical differences in the size of the animals commonly called either "burros" or "donkeys." Mules were especially sought after in Europe as working animals, as they were large, strong, and intelligent and possessed many of the best qualities of both the horse and the donkey. Because male mules are infertile, the bigger and stronger asses were, if available, bred to large European mares to produce the biggest and strongest mules possible. Over the centuries, mule breeders developed strains of especially large asses, now called "Mammoth Asses." The larger male is called a "Mammoth Jack" and his female counterpart is called a "Mammoth Jennet." The proper name for any male donkey or burro is a "jack," and the proper name for any female burro or donkey is a "jennet" (now usually nicknamed "jenny."

The practice of crossbreeding donkeys and horses to produce mules was started almost 3,000 years ago. Mules cannot breed among themselves. The male mule (called a "John") is evidently sterile, while a very few "mollies" (female mules) have given birth to a foal. The chance of a molly giving birth is very slim — close to one in a million. Breeders guess that mollies are passing on a rare horse gene and are not really producing a mule. Some breeders claim that mollies are sterile like male mules, although they do not have an explanation for the very rare births. Burros have 62 sets of chromosomes, mules have 63, and horses have 64. Whether female mules are sterile or not, it was, and is, much easier to continue the ancient practice of producing mules from a donkey and a horse. Jacks used to breed with mares are usually called "mule jacks," and jacks used to breed with jennies to procure more burros are called "jennet jacks."

A mule that is a cross between a jack (male burro) and a mare (female horse) is the only animal that should be called a "mule," as a cross between a stallion (male horse) and a jenny (female burro) is a separate hybrid called a "hinny." Most male horses are not bred with jennies (actually the stallions do not seem to want to breed with them), so hinnies are fairly rare. Hinnies and mules look alike but a hinny is more the size of a burro, while a mule is nearer to the size of a mare. Therefore a mule is usually bigger than a hinny. Another confusing practice is that jacks are called "stallions" in the United Kingdom and are sometimes referred to as such in the United States.

The trend of using large donkeys for breeding continued with the asses that were brought to the eastern United States, as European immigrant farmers sought, through selective breeding, to produce bigger and bigger donkeys. President George Washington imported the first Mammoth Jacks from Europe to the United States and kept them as breeding stock to produce mules that he used as draft animals. Some of these Mammoth Jacks were enormous — standing almost twice as high as a Spanish burro. Many of the large donkeys in the eastern United States are descended from Washington's original imports.

In contrast, the pioneers of the Southwest were generally interested in an animal that could get by with less food, and there was, for the most part, no attention paid to selective breeding. In the Southwestern part of the United States, most asses came from Mexico and were generally the descendants of animals from Spanish speaking countries in Europe; therefore they not only were smaller, hardier animals, but their owners preferred the use of the term "burro." The burros of the Spanish-speaking Mediterranean had been used (and still are used in many places around the world) for cheap and economical transportation. Usually owned by peasants, they were called "the poor man's horse or mule," and were usually put to work while still very young, as well as being constantly underfed. Both circumstances served to retard the burro's growth and keep them small.

However, whether we are considering miniature donkeys, burros, Mammoth Jacks and Jennets, or standard donkeys, they are all biologically the same animal, even though some breeders

"The Mountaineer" has a thinner and longer face than most burros.

The Burro Book, Author's Collection

in the United States believe that the term "burro" should only be used for an ass living in the wild that is a "Standard" size — thirty-six to forty-eight inches. In this book we will usually refer to the small, somewhat scruffy, but very hardy animals that were usually found around the Mediterranean (and later in Mexico and the southwestern United States) as "burros" and leave the term "donkeys" for those larger asses that were and are still generally found in the East and are generally being raised to sire bigger and stronger mules.

Whether pregnant by a horse or a jack, a jenny's term of pregnancy is about twelve months but can vary from ten and a half months to thirteen and a half months. Of course, like any animal, they can give birth prematurely. The burro's offspring that are less than one year old are called "foals" — with a male foal sometimes called a "colt" but technically being a "jack colt," and a female foal called a "filly" but technically being a "jennet foal." Jennies usually have only one foal. Very rarely (about once in 100 births) a jenny will give birth to twins, but about half the time at least one of the foals will be born dead or will die immediately after birth. Horses only have twins about 1 out of 1,000 births. About ten sets of burro twins are reported to live each year in the United States. Unless spayed or separated, burros tend to have a new foal every twelve to fifteen months because the jennies are in heat within days of giving birth to a foal.

A burro's foal will usually be born feet first and will be standing on its feet and walking within an hour of its birth. This must certainly be a carryover from their being born in the wild, when newly born foals were targeted immediately by hungry predators. A young burro can usually eat adult food within a month, although it will continue to nurse for four to nine months after its birth. At age one, the young burros are called "yearlings" and are basically the equivalent in physical development to a human teenager. However it takes until age three to five years before the burro reaches full physical and mental maturity. For this reason young burros should not be used as guard animals or lead animals until they reach that age.

Burros live to an age of thirty, forty, or even fifty years (almost twice as long as a horse), and very occasionally one might live into its sixties. The famous burro Prunes from Fairplay, Colorado, was documented to be sixty-three years old when he died. However the life expectancy of a burro that is forced to carry a heavy load (say 200 pounds or more every day) can be lowered substantially — from an average of about thirty years down to only ten or eleven.

Jacks tend to be more bossy and rambunctious than geldings (castrated jacks) or jennies, to the point that jacks are usually kept away from unsupervised, young children and are not usually used as guard animals. However both jennies and jacks were used pretty much indiscriminately by Colorado

A mother and her newborn were captured by the photographer on what was labeled "Baby's First Walk."
The Burro Book, Author's Collection

prospectors and freighters; jacks perhaps being given a slight preference because they are a little bigger than jennies and therefore can carry slightly more weight. Two jacks can get into some pretty serious fights. J. H. Lewis, in his article "Rocky Mountain Burros" described two jacks fighting, writing:

> ....*The burro rises to great heights of wrath and activity when engaged in battle with one of its own kind. Then his dull eyes flash, his ears lie back, all his shinning teeth are revealed, his hoofs fly out and he fights violently. These combats do not often occur, however. Other times the burro is one of the meekest and most faithful little burden-bearers in the world.*

Although the entire southwestern United States was greatly influence by Spain and later Mexico, for some reason the term "burro" was only widely used in Colorado, New Mexico and California. This may be due to the earlier colonization by Spain of these states, but in Texas, Nevada, Arizona, and other nearby states, the animals were usually called "donkeys" or sometimes "ships of the desert" (a term normally reserved for camels). Once the animals had been brought to what now is the United States, the conditions continued that kept them small. The main reason that Western burros were sought after, rather than mules, was that they could eat almost anything and needed no special foods, they could traverse narrow trails with sharp switchbacks (or without a trail at all), they could carry a large load (although not quite as much as mules or the eastern donkey), and they could last for days without food or water (although they do not like to go hungry and thirsty and suffer from such deprivation).

Burros come in many colors, but the most common color is gray, slate, or dun. Their colors can also be black, dark blue, brown, and shades of black and blue, sometimes with reddish tones. The burro's coat can also be white, near-white, and

These four burros show a variety of colors and markings. The largest has a bell around his neck to make it easier for his owner to find him.

The Burro Book, Author's Collection

spotted. Totally white burros were considered somewhat rare in the United States in the 1800s, but there are some parts of the Middle East where they are so common that all of the burros of a particular area might be pure white. These burros are especially sought after as symbols of purity, goodness, and sacredness. All colors are determined by the burro's winter coat, which is much heavier than in the summer.

Compared to the size of their bodies, most burros have a large head, which is very close in size to that of the much taller horse. Almost all burros have very long, dark ears, a near-white muzzle and eye rings, and near-white bellies and inner legs.

A burro's tail is only about half as long as that of a horse. It is mostly covered with short body hair except for a tassel near the very end, so it cannot swat flies as efficiently as a horse. However its hide is thicker and tougher than that of a horse, and it often rolls in dirt or sand, so it doesn't usually attract as many flies as a horse. In ancient times the burro's thick hide was prized for making shoes, sandals, and other leather items that needed to be especially durable, thick, and tough. A burro's legs are short and thin. They have chestnuts on their forelegs only, while mules and horses have chestnuts on both their hind and forelegs.

The burro's back and neck are much straighter than that of a horse, and its mane is shorter than a horse and usually thicker and straighter. The mane tends to stand straight up, like a crew cut. The texture of the burro's coat ranges from short and flat, to curly, to long and shaggy. Most burros have a cross formed by the hair on their back, which is composed of a dorsal stripe of darker hair and a dark cross stripe at the shoulders (burros do not really have withers like a horse — this area of their body is normally called "shoulders"). The dorsal cross comes from the Nubian breed of donkeys, which is now extinct. The stripes of white on the legs of some burros come from the Somalian breed.

Legend has it that the burro has the cross marking because it was the animal used by Jesus in his triumphant entry into Jerusalem, just before his crucifixion. Jesus purposely chose to ride the lowly and humble burro rather that the horse, which soldiers, kings and emperors would have used. Some Christians claim that the burro has the cross marking because it was the animal used by Mary and Jesus when Joseph and his family fled to Egypt after Jesus' birth. Supposedly Mary's burro was startled when a group of doves flew in front of the group, and the burro threw Mary and baby Jesus off its back. As a punishment, God decided that from that time forward the burro would always carry a cross on its back and that doves would always be in mourning.

Yet another legend is that the burro's cross came from the burro that carried Jesus to Jerusalem. It wished with all its heart that it could have also carried Jesus' cross to Cavalry, since the burro was a beast of burden and it would have been more proper for it to do so. As a reward for this pure love, God gave the burro the shadow of a cross on its back, which has been shared with its descendants. The burro's cross also gave rise to a popular riddle: What always carries a cross on its back but is not a Christian? Answer: A burro. The burro became so closely associated with Jesus in Europe and the Middle East that if a burro stopped and refused to move while carrying sacred objects in a Catholic country, a church was often established on that spot, as the area was considered to be especially holy.

Christopher Columbus brought the first burros to the West Indies on his second voyage to the Americas in 1495. His small herd included four jacks and two jennets. The animals were brought, in large part, to produce mules for the New World; but the intent of the Spanish was also to establish large herds of burros to be used for packing, riding, and milk production. Burro's milk had for hundreds of years been considered to be healthier than cow's milk and a remedy for different ailments such as whooping cough. A burro does not produce as much milk as a cow, because they do not need to, as their milk is much richer. Burro's milk tastes like sweetened powdered cow's milk. Because it contains a lot of fatty acids and is very high in Vitamins A, E, and F, burro's milk has been used by humans for thousands of years for dry skin and wrinkles. Cleopatra supposedly used it as a skin conditioner, and the Emperor Nero's wife often bathed in burro's milk. It is still used today as the base for many expensive skin creams and lotions.

In European folklore, whooping cough and some other respiratory ailments were said to be cured by drinking burro's milk or by cutting some of the hair from the center of the cross on the burro's back and keeping it in a pouch tied around the patient's neck. Exactly why the burro's milk and hair is supposed to cure whooping cough is unknown, but it is possible that a connection was made in ancient times because whooping cough sounds somewhat similar to the bray of certain burros. Ironically, many of the common medical problems of the burro are respiratory.

Most domestic burros are only about three to four feet high at the shoulders, although there are miniature breeds that are much smaller and large breeds of donkeys that can reach the size of a horse (about five feet at the shoulders). A standard burro weighs about half of the weight of a normal horse (about 500 to 600 pounds vs. 800 to 1,200 pounds). Today there are size categories that are sometimes used to distinguish groups of burros or donkeys. These are only "classes" of the animals and not different species or even subspecies. Officially burros less than 36 inches are "Miniature donkeys." "Standard size" is 36 inches to 48 inches. "Large standard" is 48 inches to 54 inches for jennies and 48 inches to 56 inches for jacks. Burros bigger than large standard are called "Mammoth Asses." The word "burro" is not appropriate when talking about a miniature donkey or a Mammoth Ass — the two extremes in size in the assinus family. The animal we call burros are either standard or large standard asses.

Burros are legendary for their endurance and are very strong. They can carry approximately the same weight as a horse that is twice their size. They can easily carry thirty to forty percent of their body weight for many hours at a time when they are traveling on level, smooth terrain; and they can be pushed to carry their own weight (500 to 600 pounds) in some cases. A few people even claim to have seen burros carry twice their weight for short distances, but this situation is certainly not good for the animal. Most burros can easily carry a fully grown human, although its short stature does make the situation look a little ridiculous at times.

The burro's regular load was about 150 to 300 pounds, depending on the size, age, and condition of the animal, when it was being used for long trips in hard, steep terrain like that of the mountains of Colorado. In comparison, the bigger mule could usually carry 250 to 350 pounds through the same type of terrain, but unlike the burro, a mule needed a trail to follow. Horses were very seldom used to pack freight, as they generally did not have either the stamina or the strength needed.

In the West burros were sometimes ridden instead of horses, as they were more sure-footed and hardier. They did well traveling on the steep, narrow, rocky trails and when crossing the strong, swift rivers (once they could be made to get in) of Colorado. Horses were usually used when the rider was looking for speed. A great deal of the burro's verbal abuse came from horse lovers who thought that the burro was stupid or lazy because it did not like to run fast like a horse. Many a macho man of the Old West would not ride a burro because they thought a man looked silly riding an animal with such short legs. A burro does have a great distaste for speed, but just because they do not like to go fast does not mean they are lazy or that they cannot move quickly if they want to do so. With short, little legs, the burro might just realize it is not going to win a sprint, but its stamina is something that it can count on. In this respect, the burro and

Burros were sometimes used to pull wagons. In this case four have been hitched, perhaps to pull a heavy load.
The Burro Book, Author's Collection

the horse are kind of like the tortoise and the hare — the burro might not get to its destination fast, but it will surely get there.

Although J. H. Lewis obviously preferred to go faster than a burro's normal pace, he was impressed with the burro's sure-footedness:

> *His slowness and sureness of movement enable (the burro) to go up and over the loftiest mountain summits, the rockiest curves, and on the narrowest of trails. He plods sleepily along on the very edge of the most frightful precipice without once losing his head, or making a single mistake. He goes fearlessly along when his other relative, the horse, would not go if he could.*

Rev. George Darley felt that burros were:

> *... a safe way of traveling, considering the roughness of the terrain. No one feared being wrecked by a misplaced switch or a broken rail. Having our provisions and blankets, we were independent travelers.*

There are several reasons that the burro is more sure-footed than a horse or mule. Their hooves are much smaller and more rounded, and they are more careful about where they place them. Their eyes are further apart than a horse and this allows them to see all four of their feet as they touch the ground. The burro's hooves are also not as brittle as those of a horse. They are more elastic, which gives them better traction, but which also makes it important to keep the hooves of the burro trimmed when it is not being used regularly. The hooves of an unkempt burro that does not walk regularly have been reported to grow to over a foot long. A horse must be shod if used for transportation, but neither a mule nor a burro needs iron shoes, unless they are worked extensively in rough, rocky terrain. Of course, most of the terrain where they were used in Colorado is rough and rocky.

A burro will bite or kick at a person, but usually less than a mule or horse. Biting, kicking, and running are their natural defense mechanisms when they feel threatened or in danger. They also sometimes "nip" when they are playing with people, but they can be taught not to do so. That they only nip when playing is not much consolation to the human they nip — it still hurts. Burros are generally gentler and calmer than most horses and mules, but if a man ever sees a burro's ears flatten back and the burro shows his teeth, the man had better get out of the way fast!

When asked why he preferred burros to horses, freighter Jim Wheeler said:

> For one thing, they have more sense. You never have to worry none about a burro getting locoed (eating loco weed). They wouldn't eat the stuff. They could go two or three days, if necessary without water…. Another thing was the way they feed on most anything. I'd just turn them a-loose at night and then find them within a couple hundred yards or so from camp in the morning, ready to go again. A horse would have half starved to death, or strayed off so far that it would have taken a week to reach him with a postcard!

Burros, however, do prefer to eat food that is good for them if they are given a choice; but not only do burros not have to have special grains (or even hay) like horses, but they are immune to many of the diseases that attack horses, or at the very least are not affected as badly. Besides respiratory problems, burros, like other animals, are subject to some disease, infection, and parasites. However, they are much more likely to suffer in silence, which has given rise to the inference that they are less likely to have these ailments. Since burros came from the desert country of Africa, they can go a long time without water (two to four days depending on the conditions). In fact, they can live longer without water than any pack animal in the world except for the camel. In the mountains of Colorado, water can usually be found pretty easily; but the burro's keen ability to smell water was a very important factor for the prospector when working in dry land areas. Since the burro can smell water from far off, it can take its owner, as well as the other domesticated animals that might be with them, to a water hole.

Burros are very hardy, and they have survived some amazing accidents. One baby burro was reported to fall sixty feet into the Gunnison River and was not injured at all. A burro that was packing flour on the Bear Creek Trail near Ouray, Colorado, fell 200 feet off a cliff. The weight of the flour turned the burro heels upwards as it fell, so that it landed on the flour sacks. It was reportedly unhurt, although it was pretty "shook up." Several burros have been reported to have survived dynamite explosions that killed their masters. This usually happened when a prospector was warming dynamite over a stove. It sounds crazy, but frozen sticks of dynamite would not explode and often had to be warmed before they could be used in the winter.

Owners of burros are also quick to point out that the burro has a larger head and therefore must have a proportionately larger brain than a horse or a mule; and, accordingly, they must therefore be smarter than those animals. In actuality, just as with humans, each burro has its own personality, intelligence, and own responses to different events; so we can only generalize about their characteristics. Burros are usually very intelligent but rather complex. In the early days, it took a good burro puncher some time to recognize each individual burro's habits and traits, and today it still takes a good amount of time and patience to get a burro to change its behavior, if that can be done at all.

There have been many false reports about the personalities and temperament of burros that have given them a bad name and have carried over into today's slang. For example, we use the word "jackass" for someone who is obnoxious, rude, and thoughtless. This personality is about as far from that of a burro as possible. We also use the word "dumbass" for someone who is stupid or ignorant; again it is a complete contradiction to the intelligence of burros. Even the term "asinine" comes from "ass-like" and means stupid or silly, while the burro is neither. Horses seem to be the glamorous mounts; while burros are the tireless little workers — something like Cinderella, except the burro has never been given a chance to go to the ball. Horses often carried soldiers into the "glory" of battle, but just as importantly, the burros usually came right behind them carrying food, water, and supplies for the men and their horses.

Burros are a legendary animal from a personality point of view — sober, patient, enduring, humorous, courageous, and strong-hearted. They are said to "accept their lowly lot in life without any attempt at rebellion." However, as one man said, "to reason with a burro is as vain as to try to reason with one's mother-in-law." Burros know they are smart and they act like it. Burros thrive on affection and attention, and as another writer put it, they are "grateful for the slightest gesture of sincerity and kindness." Although it is sometimes hard to understand, burros also have a good sense of humor.

A lot of what is considered to be stubbornness in the burro is actually justified fear or a very high and reasonable sense of self-preservation. As compared to the horse, the burro has always had to depend more on its wits rather than its speed. It has also been forced to rely on itself for self preservation on almost all occasions throughout history. The burro was often left to roam in harsh weather and in areas filled with predators, rather than being kept safe in corrals and stables like mules or horses. As a result, the burro is more wary and can sense predators and other forms of danger more easily than a horse. Burros are curious, and when they sense danger they become very careful. It might take them a little while to figure out what course of action they wish to take, but once they decide they will usually stick with it.

Even the dictionary describes the burro as "patient but stubborn." In reality they are just thoughtful and cautious. For example, a horse can be made to put itself into a dangerous situation (such as crossing a raging river), but not a burro. Burros prefer to do what is best for themselves, which is not always the same as what their human owner is trying to get them to do. The burro is not usually being stubborn if it balks at a stream — it is merely questioning who is smarter, it or the human.

Another example of obeying or not obeying may be in order. Burros have all of the gaits of horses, and some have even been entered in professional racing and jumping contests. However, a burro does not like to gallop unless it is absolutely necessary, because it is a tiring and dangerous gait. This can be a decided advantage for its rider. As one man put it, "I would rather get to my intended destination slowly than get to the hospital fast." The same goes for jumping over an object. To the burro it just looks like a good way to get hurt. However, a burro can usually be coaxed to do almost anything with food. No amount of whipping or punching will make a burro go where he doesn't want to go, but a small cube of sugar or a cabbage leaf will almost always work.

One other very important personality trait is that it is hard to make burros panic. They will usually think a situation through before taking action — a characteristic that serves them well when acting as guard animals. Burros are very inquisitive and alert. They are almost always the first animal in a pasture that detects the presence of trouble, and they are very brave and courageous when danger is encountered. They will usually stand and fight even a bear or wolf and will usually chase them away. Because of this trait burros have been, and still are, used to help protect herds of cattle, sheep, and goats, which are notorious for doing nothing or going into total panic when predators are near.

One example of the calm personality of the burro was given by J. H. Lewis:

> He is serenely indifferent to the things that affright the soberest horse. At his very first sight of a locomotive under full headway, the donkey might prick up his ears slightly, and the sleepy look in his eyes might give way to mild curiosity, but all the puffing and screeching (of the locomotive) will not make (the burro) run away.

However Lewis had to disparage the little burro — "This calm indifference is, I fear, more the result of stupidity than courage."

The burro's alarm is its voice, which is so loud, raspy and brassy, that it not only sounds a signal of danger but often scares away predators. Because burros are very good at defending themselves, they have only two natural enemies in present-day Colorado — the mountain lion and a pack of coyotes; and burros have been known to fight off even these predators when they or their foals were threatened.

Burros make a very loud and unique bray (rightly described as "Aw-Hee" but sometimes described as" Hee-Haw"), which can be heard for over two miles. It has been said that the burro's bray sounds like what Gabriel's trumpet on judgment day. One person described their bray as "a protest against the harshness of their fate." Jacks seem to love braying more than jennies and will usually start with any opportunity (such as the sun coming up or the wind rustling a leaf). Their bray has earned them the nicknames of the "Rocky Mountain Canary," the "Colorado Mockingbird," or the "Rocky Mountain Nightingale." One Colorado legislator with a good sense of humor even suggested that the lark bunting be dropped as the Colorado state bird and be replaced by the Rocky Mountain Canary. The motion was ruled out of order before a vote could be taken.

The burro has five identified sounds — a bray, grunt, growl, snort, and wuffle. The burro's bray can have different tones that express emotions like anger, happiness, love, sadness, and fear. The different emotions are usually recognized after a while by the burro's owner and can give great insight into what is going on within its mind. It also has "a half crying, half sniffling plea for a treat" that only a person with a heart of stone could ignore.

Since burros had to become well-adapted to arid and semi-arid climates, through evolution they have gained unique traits that help them cope with life in the desert, and which are also of great advantage in the mountains. In the wild, burros usually live separate from each other or in pairs (as opposed to the tight-knit, large herds of wild horses). The burro's long ears help it hear other burros at a great distance, and help keep it cool because of the large blood supply present in their large ears. Their white noses and underbellies also helped to reflect the desert sun's rays and keep them cooler.

Donkeys and burros in the wild (called "feral" animals, although that term is technically reserved for animals that have been domesticated but later went into the wild, as opposed to an animal that had always been wild) are quick to defend themselves with a very strong kick of the hind legs, biting, and striking out with their front legs. Horses usually run when scared, but burros have learned to stand and fight, as they know they are not fast enough to get away from most predators. In many cases, they will hide when danger approaches. Burros also have keen eye-sight and a range of vision that is greater than a horse. Rarely are they bitten by a rattlesnake, because they usually see and hear the snake while they are still some distance away from it. Their acute eyesight also comes in handy for their "sentry duties."

And then there is the burro's incredible digestive system, which was a necessity in the deserts of Africa and allows it, if necessary, to eat almost any type of vegetation (such as cacti and thistles) and efficiently extract moisture from food. This

"Mama's Baby" clearly shows the short, coarse "crew-cut" mane of the mother.

The Burro Book, Author's Collection

situation probably came about because historically horses and other large animals in the wild tended to take over the better pasture such as in a low lying area. Burros were forced to move into the hills and cliffs where the forage was sparser. They eat less food than a horse of equal size and weight and even get sick if they are fed too much food or some types of grains. European, African, and Spanish peasants fed their burros scraps, leftovers, and spoiled food, or allowed them to roam and scavenge for whatever garbage, grass, or weeds they could find.

Many Colorado prospectors were at the other end of the feeding spectrum and loved to feed their burros flapjacks (pancakes) and biscuits, often covered with molasses. Hungry burros, like goats, have been reported to eat clothing, sticks, bark, and even tin cans. Like goats, they are really eating the paper off the cans or looking for something left inside. However, as one writer noted, they seem to prefer the cans with pictures of corn, carrots and other vegetables on the label. Burros also seem to have a sixth sense that helps them avoid naturally growing poisonous plants like locoweed, which can kill or otherwise play havoc with horses and other domesticated animals.

Burros are very social, both among themselves and with humans. Today some breeders will not sell an animal unless they know that another burro will be kept with it. Perhaps in the pioneer days the prospector made a good substitute. On the other hand, it has been written that burros have experienced enough of human behavior to know when to be wary and when to love us. There are also times when a burro just does not want humans around it, and a good owner will come to recognize these signs.

When the burros of today are treated well and a trust is established between them and their owners, they usually seek out attention and love being groomed by their masters. Coupled with their patience and intelligence, burros often become pets

This pinto jennet has had an almost pure white foal, but its color could change as it gets older.
The Burro Book, Author's Collection

to their families; this was true even thousands of years ago. However in more recent times this friendship and companionship has sometimes been forgotten by man. Frank Brookshier explained the burro's outlook on life well:

> They do not expect anything beyond the necessities of life, though they are not adverse to a few comforts.... To these animals luxury is the love and attention of its owner.

CHAPTER TWO

℃⊙℃

The Burro Comes to America
The Heritage of the Spanish

The story of the burro in America begins with the second voyage of Christopher Columbus in 1495, resumes with the Spanish conquest of the Mexica (a culture also known as the "Aztecs" in what is now the country of Mexico), and continues with the Spanish exploration and settlement of what has become the southwestern part of the United States. Many Americans living in the twenty-first century do not know of the enormous influence that the Spanish (and later the Mexicans) had on the formation of the United States, especially in the Southwest, and the crucial part that the burro played in the Spanish destiny.

Most historians agree that the introduction by the Spanish of domesticated beasts of burden was the single most beneficial contribution that any country made to the existing Native American cultures during the European discovery and conquest of the American continents, which dates back to the early

1500s. As Charles Lummis wrote in his book *Flowers of Our Lost Romance*:

> *The Spanish introduction of the horse, mule, burro and ox to America marked the longest stride that so many people, in so short a time, have ever taken....*

Lummis also believed the burro rather than the horse was the most important of all the animals carried by the Spanish to New Spain (there were dozens of other non-indigenous animals brought by the Spanish, the chicken probably being the most common today). Lummis wrote further:

> *Two-thirds of the New World would not be civilized yet (in 1896).... The burro has been the cornerstone of history and the father of civilization....*

The burro was first brought, along with other European livestock, to islands in the Caribbean on Columbus' second voyage. To keep the burros and mules that he was transporting from getting hurt, and to keep them under control during the long, dangerous ocean voyage, they were kept in hammocks hung in the ship's hold, with only their back feet touching the floor. All of the animals survived the voyage without a problem.

It was several more years before burros arrived on the mainland of the Americas. They had to wait until 1523 for the total conquest of the Aztec nation by the Spanish conquistadors, who used the horse very effectively in their battles with the native population. The first burros probably stepped onto the North American continent proper in New Spain (the area that is now known as Mexico). They were brought by Juan de Zumarraga, the first Roman Catholic Bishop of New Spain, who was appointed in 1528, and who brought two pairs of burros with him. By the next year, Zumarraga was recommending to Spain that a large breeding herd of burros be established. He made this suggestion in large part because he was trying to help the enslaved native people, as he had been designated by the church as "Protector of the Native Indians" and took this job very seriously. He knew that burros could assume much of the exhausting and heavy freighting work that was then being done on the backs of the conquered Native Americans. This mode of freighting was not new; it had been done this way among the Aztec themselves for hundreds of years.

Zumarraga also needed the burro as the "workhorse" of the Spanish padres, who had already begun to spread out over New Spain to preach the Christian gospel and do what they felt was God's work in this new land. The dependable burro was not only good transportation for the padres but was also a very fitting Christian symbol for the friars, as it was of humble origin, was very loving and peaceful, and had been chosen as a mount by Jesus himself. Efforts to establish the burro went well, and soon the little animal could be found in most of central and southern New Spain, although it had not yet stepped foot into the territory to the far north that would eventually become the United States.

The burro was quickly recognized by the natives to be a superior pack animal — a fact already well-known by the Spanish. Burros could carry a heavy weight for their size and were patient, dependable, and in an emergency even a good source of food. Within thirty years of their arrival on the mainland of the continent, burros were fairly plentiful and well enough established in New Spain that they were being sold in the open markets; and, as one of the main sources of transportation, they had helped to virtually eliminate the human "pack mules." Antonio Mendoza, Viceroy of New Spain in 1550, wrote that "a well-behaved jenny has to be groomed in order to bring fifteen to twenty pesos," so in addition to being traded, burros were also being sold in the open market at a fairly low price. They were evidently also doing a good job at their task of producing mules, as there were also many more of those hardy animals in New Spain.

Burros were often used in the 1700s and 1800s to carry firewood, which sold for about twenty-five cents per burro load.
The Burro Book, Author's Collection

In the meantime, Spanish ships had been sailing around the tip of South America since 1525 and working their way up the Pacific coast to colonize the western parts of New Spain. Once Spanish ports were established on the Pacific and the Atlantic coasts, more pack animals were needed to transport large loads of freight to Mexico City, the capital of New Spain, and overland routes established and used by large pack trains of mules, burros, and ox carts traveling between the eastern ports of Veracruz and Portobello to Acapulco and other cities on the western coast. There freight and passengers were reloaded on to Spanish ships going all over the Pacific. In addition, Spanish ships frequently arrived from across the Pacific, bringing trade goods from Asia and the Philippines, and transporting goods like silk and spices that went overland to the east coast and then on to Spain and Europe.

It was not long before valuable minerals, such as gold and silver, were being mined in New Spain and transported down from the mountains on the backs of burros and mules to the port cities on the Gulf Coast to be taken back to Spain. Even "specialty" items like apples were carried on burro's backs. Supposedly, these lowly pack animals were sometimes shod with shoes made of gold or silver, because those metals were cheaper and more available in New Spain than iron. They may have been cheap, but because gold and silver are such soft metals, this seems to be a colorful but unlikely tale. Most of these animals were worked in pack trains (called "Las Conductas" or "The Pipeline") or driven in herds on trails that were just as rugged and steep as any that would later be traveled by burros in Colorado.

When the burros were no longer able to work because of age or injury, they were usually too tough and beaten up (or perhaps more sentimentally "too loved") to eat, so they were often released into the wild to fend for themselves. Most could have found enough food or water, but many fell prey to wolves and other predators. However some animals survived long enough to sire offspring, and it was not long before New Spain had a fairly large feral burro population. Burros were becoming numerous enough in New Spain by the late 1500s that many wild burros were only hunted for their meat.

As the Spanish slowly, over the next few centuries, pushed their frontier to the north through today's Mexican deserts, the burro was almost always with them. After all, the burro was descended from animals that had thrived in the deserts of northern Africa, so they were well-adapted to this task. They not only traveled with the Spanish conquistadors, but burros were also being used by peasants for farming, gathering firewood, and taking farm products to market in the settlements that were founded along the way.

Normally there would have been no reason for the Spanish to push into this barren, basically waterless country to the north (the Spanish called the land "El Norte"), but many of those men going north from Mexico City in the first half of the sixteenth century were Spanish conquistadors, riding their fine and elegantly decorated horses, and looking for gold. They were especially enticed by rumors of a province called "Cibola," said to contain the "Seven Cities of Cibola" or the "Seven Cities of Gold." There was nothing concrete about these rumors, but they were very persistent, even though ever-changing. The rumors varied radically from a golden treasure accumulated by the Native Americans to riches from Europe taken to Cibola by seven bishops and members of the Spanish royal family, who supposedly were fleeing Spain ahead of the conquering armies of the Moors. Sometimes the reports mentioned seven cities and sometimes it was seven caves filled with gold. The details changed constantly, but one fact was always the same — there was supposedly a lot of gold to be found far to the north of Mexico City.

These rumors were given some substantiation by Cabeza de Vaca and Esteban, his Moorish slave, who were two of only four men of a 600-man expeditionary group who made it across the entire southwest to the Pacific Coast and then down to Mexico City. There they reported to the Spanish authorities that they had heard about Cibola and that it was an actual city that even had houses and streets made of solid gold! In 1539 Franciscan Friar Marcos de Niza and Esteban were sent north with a small group of men to follow up on the Cibola rumors. Esteban was killed, but De Niza reported back and told authorities that he had actually seen Cibola (although from a great distance) and that the city shimmered like gold.

It did not take long for the Spanish to react to this news. Fransico Vasquez de Coronado left Mexico City on February 23, 1540, with the first formal expedition into what is now Arizona and New Mexico. It was a huge group of over 1,000 men and thousands of animals. Coronado eventually decided that the Zuni pueblos (near today's Arizona-New Mexico border) must be the Seven Cities of Cibola, but determined that Cibola's "golden" walls were made of adobe and not precious gold. He returned to Mexico City in shame. Coronado's expedition contained horses and mules (many of which he lost along the way), but it is not known if the group had burros with them. If so, they would have been the first burros in North America. After Coronado's disaster, Spain did not make another major push north for over a half a century.

Ironically, just a little north of where Coronado stopped looking for Cibola are the San Juan Mountains of extreme northwestern New Mexico and Southwestern Colorado. Over 300 years later, huge quantities of gold and silver were mined from the San Juans. Although cities made of gold or caves filled with gold have never been found, the remains of extremely old mining prospects were discovered in the San Juans by early American prospectors. Did some early Spanish expeditions make it to their Cibola? Did they at least dig for and take away large quantities of gold? Had the Pueblo Indians or the Aztec mined here for gold at one time? If the Spanish were there, they almost certainly used burros; but no one yet knows the answer to these questions.

Meanwhile, Spain continued its efforts to build up the number of burros in New Spain. In 1561 twelve jennies and three jacks were brought to the mainland from Cuba. They were evidently the first breeding burros that were delivered for the express purpose of producing burro offspring. The object was to have burros spread out among every frontier outpost of New Spain. At least one jack and jenny were to go to each outlying settlement, so as to encourage a rapid rise in the number of burros. Since the burro population can double every four years, it was a very good plan.

Although he was not the first Spanish explorer to venture into what is now the United States, Juan de Onate became the first Spaniard to head north with explicit orders from the Spanish crown (King Phillip II) to colonize the area that would eventually become New Mexico. Searching for precious metals was, of course, another of his goals. It is well-documented that Onate had numerous burros with his group. He had started assembling his expedition at his father's silver mine in December, 1596, and he evidently had been given or bought some of his expedition's burros from his father's operation, as burros had now been used at various mining operations in New Spain for over fifty years.

Onate's expedition spent a long time organizing before it finally moved to the north in 1598. He personally took thirty

Mexican boys carried water in large pottery jars, and in this photo another boy is on this burro's back.
The Burro Book, Author's Collection

mules and burros on the expedition, and many of the colonists who were going to settle in the new country brought their own burros with them. Most of the eight priests and three lay brothers in the expedition also brought burros. Onate and his huge entourage therefore were the first people that we know for sure brought burros into what is now the United States. We do not know the total number of burros that were included in Onate's expedition, but we do know that his inventory of supplies (which had to be prepared for the Spanish crown to show that he was capable of accomplishing his task) included almost 1,000 burro shoes.

Onate headed north and crossed the Rio Grande River near the present-day cities of El Paso, Texas and Juarez, Mexico. There, on April 30, 1598, he claimed for God, the King, and himself all of the adjoining lands drained by the Rio Grande River. Although he never saw it, he had officially claimed a good part of what would become south central Colorado. Onate continued north, visiting and making friends with the many Pueblo Indians that he encountered along the way. Onate eventually made it as far north as the junction of the Chama and the Rio Grande Rivers (in the area around the Taos Pueblo, New Mexico), only about forty miles from today's New Mexico-Colorado border.

Near the junction of these two rivers, Onate in 1599 established the capital of the new Province of New Mexico, which he named "San Gabriel de Yungue." This was the first purely Spanish settlement in New Mexico and the second (Jamestown was first) European settlement in the land that is now the United States. Earlier however, some of Onate's people had stayed and settled at some of the existing pueblos along the Rio Grande River. Many of these settlers had burros with them.

There is no record of Onate going into Colorado; but members of his party did. They looked for seven caves that were supposedly filled with gold near the headwaters of the Rio Grande River; but like Coronado they had no success, even though they were in the gold and silver rich San Juan Mountains of today's

Southwest Colorado. Even after his settlers were established, Onate continued to send small parties out looking for gold and silver. They could be called the first prospectors in Colorado, and they undoubtedly had burros with them, which would have been the first in Colorado.

The Pueblo Indians whom Onate met during his travels all loved the gentle little burro, which was quite different from the feisty horses and mules that had been brought by Francisco Vasquez de Coronado. Burros matched with the Pueblo Indian's slow and easy-going temperament better and were of much more use to them than the horse. Evidently some of the little animals were traded or stolen by these Indians, as the burro was soon a common sight in all the Pueblo villages along the Rio Grande River.

Winter was approaching, and the Onate expedition was facing the real possibility of starving to death. Onate demanded supplies from the Acoma Pueblo — supplies that the natives could not give up without putting their own people in danger of a famine. When Onate persisted, the Acoma Pueblo rebelled and killed eleven of his soldiers, including Onate's nephew and two of his servants. Onate's revenge was overwhelming and unnecessarily brutal. He attacked the Pueblo, killing 800 villagers, enslaving 500 women and children, and cutting off the left foot of twenty-four men who had surrendered. Onate gave up further exploration soon thereafter and went back to Mexico City, but there were small groups of priests, settlers, and prospectors that stayed behind in the Province of New Mexico.

Onate may have had personal failure because of his actions, but there was now a small toehold of Spanish settlers established in New Mexico, many of whom had burros; and Onate had extended the central El Camino Real (The King's Highway) 600 to 700 additional miles to the north. By 1609 this road ran a total of about 1,800 miles from Mexico City to the new capital of the Province of New Mexico — Santa Fe. It is the oldest road of such length in the United States, and within ten year after

Onate's visit, burros were constantly traveling El Camino Real to bring supplies to the settlers in New Mexico. The pack trains of burros that traveled over it (along with mules and ox carts) might have included as few as five or as many as 500 animals, usually tended by one man for every five animals.

El Camino Real was not only a very important road for New Spain, but a crucial part of the Province of New Mexico's development. It was virtually the only route for settlers to get themselves, equipment, trade goods, and supplies into the new province until the Old Spanish Trail and the Santa Fe Trail were developed over 200 years later. By 1609 committees were being formed in Mexico City to determine what should be shipped to the Spanish friars in New Mexico Province and by what methods merchandise was to be transported. A huge convoy was then sent out every three years with these items. In between, hundreds of smaller groups and traders used the road. On the way back the burros and mules carried salt, wool

Six Hopi boys and girls ride their burros while being watched over by an older adult in the 1900s.

The Burro Book, Author's Collection

blankets, copper, silver, and turquoise. Unfortunately, the road was also used to bring hundreds of Indian slaves to the gold and silver mines of Mexico. Later there was another El Camino Royale established to supply the Spanish missions that were being opened in California.

In the mid-1600s several missions were established in the Province of New Mexico, and during most of the middle part of the seventeenth century there was a constant power struggle going on between the Spanish church and the Spanish government in "El Norte." Spain wanted to build its empire — part of which meant gaining the support of the local population. However the church wanted Christian converts and had little tolerance for any vestige of the old Pueblo religions or traditions. The natives greatly resented the destruction of their way of life, and (combined with the memory of what had happened at the Acoma Pueblo massacre) on August 10, 1680, open conflict erupted.

During the "Pueblo Revolt," pueblo people killed eighteen priests, three lay brothers, and 380 Spaniards, including many women and children. The remaining Spaniards fled to Santa Fe and the friendly Isleta Pueblo, but soon continued their fast retreat down the Rio Grande River to El Paso. Almost all of the Spanish livestock was left behind, and New Mexico was soon under the control of the Pueblo Indians. The Native Americans were ordered by their leader, Pope, to destroy all vestiges of the Spanish way of life, including the livestock, which would have meant that the domesticated herds that had slowly been built up over almost a hundred years would have been exterminated. However these animals were evidently too important to the Pueblo people to be killed, and later indications were that most horses, cattle, mules, oxen and burros were not slaughtered, but instead were confiscated and hidden for later use. Within months, the Pueblo Indians were fighting among themselves and had splintered into many factions.

In 1692 the Spanish under Don Diego de Vargas reoccupied the Province of New Mexico. There was some fighting, but most Pueblo Indians surrendered without resistance. Within two years all of New Mexico was resettled by Spain and was at peace again. De Vargas went north into the San Luis Valley in today's Colorado as part of his activity, and the San Luis Valley

Diego and his burro pose in front of a bread-making oven in the Pueblo of Taos.

The Burro Book Author' Collection

and the Sangre de Cristo Mountains were named by members of his expedition. By the early 1700s domesticated livestock were again common among the Spanish, this time including sheep and goats, as well as mules, horses, and burros. Burros and mules were now packing wool and the many new crops being raised in New Mexico.

Burros continued to be very popular among the Pueblo Indians, and they were especially useful for carrying water and firewood, both of which were often quite some distance from the pueblos. However there was a negative side to all this — the burros were often getting into trouble, especially when they ate the Native American's growing crops. The burros were too important to be killed, but the Pueblos established a custom of cutting off part of the ear of the offending animal, so that every-

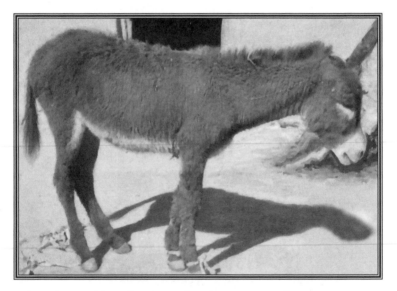

When the Pueblo Indians caught a burro eating their growing crops, they cut off a part of its ear to let others know that the burro should be watched. This burro has entirely lost one ear because of repeated theft.

The Burro Book, Author's Collection

one would know it was a mischievous burro and could keep an eye on it. Some burros were known to have had both of their ears entirely cut off — one little piece at a time.

The Pueblo tribes were not alone in Native American utilization of burros. The Navajo also kept burros with their sheep, not only to help guard them from predators, but also to help the sheep find water and green grass, while assisted by the burro's keen sense of smell. It reportedly took only a few weeks to train a burro to do all the tasks needed to watch over and guide a flock of sheep; and when the sheep were sheared, the burros were used to take the wool, or rugs and blankets made from their wool, to market.

In the 1700s ranching and farming flourished along the bigger rivers of New Mexico. Both Santa Fe and Albuquerque became major early-day trading centers, and burros could be seen everywhere in these two towns. However, Native Americans, other than the Pueblo and Navajo, were much more warlike and began to harass the Spanish ranchers and farmers. The horse culture had spread rapidly through the native tribes of the West; and Native American raiders were now coming into New Mexico from hundreds of miles away.

By the late-1700s the Spanish decided that they had had enough of the raiding Native Americans, and they established an aggressive program to defeat unfriendly tribes. In 1779 Juan Baptiste de Anza traveled north to face the Comanche led by Cuerno Verde. De Anza decisively defeated the Comanche and Cuerno Verde was killed. De Anza's huge party (573 soldiers plus an equal number of Utes and Apaches) included many mules and burros that were transporting supplies for the expedition through the San Luis Valley and Arkansas River Valley.

Later, while out looking for raiding hostile tribes to the west of New Mexico, De Anza explored much of what is now southern Arizona and California (traveling all the way up the coast from Los Angeles to Monterrey and San Francisco). Shortly after these expeditions, he became the governor of New Mexico and attempted to connect the two colonies. The Spanish settlements in California had not developed as quickly as in New Mexico, but by 1769 the Spanish were seriously beginning to occupy California, in great part due to Russian threats to do the same. Prior to this time, the Spanish had explored California mainly with ships that sailed along the Pacific Coast, and very few settlers were taken to California to colonize the land lying beyond the coast.

Unlike California, by the mid-eighteenth century Spanish settlers had occupied much of what is now New Mexico, and burros had become plentiful in the area. There were feral burros, as well as the many burros that had been established among the Navajo and the Pueblo Indian tribes. The agrarian Pueblo and Navajo Indians were also using the burro as a form of human transportation, especially for long trips. However other Native American tribes continued to show disdain for the burro, preferring the much faster horse for their mounts. The burro returned the insult, as it seemed to have an innate dislike of these "horse-loving" Native Americans and was always on the lookout for them. This made the burro a great "early warning system" when there were "Indian problems."

By the late eighteenth century the Spanish were aggressively trying to get settlers to locate somewhere other than along the banks of the Rio Grande and other major rivers in New Mexico. To accomplish this, land grants were established in areas all the way up into Colorado. Large numbers of burros, horses, and mules were raised on most of the resulting ranches, with many of these animals being raised to sell.

There was also an active push to establish missions, as well as farms and ranches on the Pacific Coast; and there were many "part-time" Spanish prospectors working small-time silver and turquoise mining operations in what would become California, Arizona, New Mexico, and Colorado. Besides silver, some gold and turquoise was found in the mountains of Colorado along the lower San Luis Valley; the King and Hall Mines being the most famous.

Several very important events that affected what is today's Colorado happened in the early nineteenth century. The United States bought the Louisiana Territory from France in 1803 with the border between New Spain and the newly acquired territory set at the Arkansas River. This meant that most of what became northeast Colorado became a part of the United States. Up until this time France and Spain had been the only countries with a real interest in what became Colorado. Now they were joined by the aggressively expanding United States.

Another event going on during this time was the Mexican War of Independence, which began in September, 1810, and lasted until 1821. The war started as a peasant revolt against the Spanish colonials, and waivered back and forth for years with mainly guerilla warfare. After winning its freedom, Mexico became a nation — although it was a very poor nation. Spain had begun to realize the potential value of what would eventually become the American southwest and began to pump a few trade goods into New Mexico and California by 1800. After 1821 Mexico was much more aggressive in encouraging trade with the United States and in allowing foreign traders and trappers into its country. The border between the two countries remained at the Arkansas River, but many Americans traveled into that portion of Mexico that is now southern Colorado and New Mexico.

Yet another force was set in motion at the conclusion of the Mexican War of Independence. Captain William Becknell of the United States opened the Santa Fe Trail that originated in present-day Kansas City, Missouri, in September and October of 1821. Every item on that first trip came in on the back of horses and mules (wagons were not used until the second trip). Becknell found the main or northern branch of the Santa Fe Trail to be difficult enough that he went back on what came to be called the "Cimarron Cutoff." According to George Sibley, early U. S. Road Commissioner, Becknell came into Santa Fe on horses, but left with mules and burros bringing Spanish trade goods back to Missouri.

Coming from the east, the Cimarron Route split from the main trail at the point that became Dodge City, staying out of the mountains, but passing through a land where grass was very sparse, waterholes were long distances apart, and there was a general lack of wildlife. This made the Cimarron Cutoff less popular with many travelers, although it was shorter, cutting about ten days off the two month trip. If taken, it included the perfect conditions and terrain for using burros, so they were often seen on this route, especially traveling east. Both basic routes of the main Santa Fe Trail had been a series of Indian trails for years before Becknell traveled them, but they were not heavily traveled until the new country of Mexico welcomed foreign trade. Only a few hardy Americans, French, and English had been over the trail before 1800 in unsuccessful attempts to trade with Spain. Most of the early travelers walked the trail, carrying their trade goods on their backs. After it was used for a while, the main route was traveled mostly by wagons belonging to big trading companies and pulled by mules. Burros were usually only seen with the smaller groups.

The Santa Fe Trail was important enough to the United States that in 1825 Congress voted to use federal funds to protect the entire route, even though much of the trail was in Mexican territory. Many travelers in the small caravans used Eastern donkeys, burros, or oxen on the trail because they were less likely to be stolen by raiding Indians than were horses or mules. The Santa Fe Trail opened up a second route for trade goods coming into New Mexico. Thousands of Americans were to eventually travel the 800-mile trail, although it was used primarily for commercial and military traffic. Manufactured goods went west and wool, furs, horses, donkeys, and mules went back to the East.

By 1830 burros, mules, and horses were also traveling a third major trade route along the 1,200 mile trail from Santa Fe, New Mexico to Los Angeles, California, which came to be called the "Old Spanish Trail." Wagons were not used much on this route,

*This 1852 sketch of Cochetopa Pass on the North Branch of the
Old Spanish Trail may be the earliest illustration of burros in
Colorado.*

Sketch by R. H. Kern, Author's Collection

because it was very rough and steep in places. The founding of the trail is officially credited to Antonio Armijo, who made the first round-trip journey with sixty men and 100 mules in 1829. He traded blankets and other items made of wool for horses, which were relatively inexpensive in California — in fact many were just running in wild herds. The main route ran north out of Santa Fe, so as to avoid the Mohave Desert and extremely hostile Native Americans that were directly to the west of Santa Fe. The trail then went northwest into today's extreme southern Colorado and into central Utah, where it turned to the southwest through Utah, Arizona, Nevada, and into California. The opening of the trail was a very important event, as it meant that Santa Fe had a third way of getting needed supplies — and this route ended at the Pacific Ocean, where Santa Fe merchants could trade for foreign goods. Soon, not only traders but prospectors, emigrants, outlaws, and trappers traveled the trail, and it was also a favorite route for horse thieves and Indian slave traders. This route was heavily used from 1830 until the Mexican-American War started.

The Old Spanish Trail had a second branch called the "Northern" or "Mountain Branch" of the Old Spanish Trail, which ran from Taos north through the San Luis Valley, over Cochetopa Pass, and then proceeded west down the Gunnison and Colorado Rivers into Utah. The two branches met at the Green River in Utah. Large numbers of burros were used on both of these trails, and these pack animals and their descendants were to become a major source of burros when American prospectors "discovered" Colorado in 1859.

With all this new trading, it did not take long before Santa Fe was booming and there was even a spot called "Burro Alley" in the city. It was really more like a block-long street that contained some of the roughest saloons, gambling halls, and houses of prostitution in Santa Fe. It got its name from the many traders, trappers, freighters, and burro punchers who would take time to stop and "talk shop" in the street, sometimes leaving

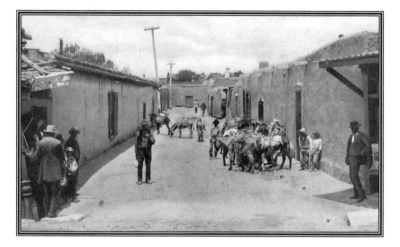

Burro Alley in Santa Fe (seen here about 1885) was a place for freighters (most of whom used burros) to stop, talk shop, and have a drink in the adjacent saloons.

The Burro Book, Author's Collection

their burros in the road while the men had some fun. Burro Alley provided a place for men to learn of new jobs or gold discoveries, talk about common problems, sell firewood that had been collected, and so forth. It truly earned its name — it was always full of burros.

In 1836 Texas gained its independence from Mexico and claimed a good part of what is now Colorado as part of the Republic of Texas. During the Mexican-American War of 1846-48, the United States took all the land that is now New Mexico and Colorado essentially without conflict. General Stephen W. Kearney and his "Army of the West" (300 cavalry and 1600 foot soldiers) simply occupied the territory. Kearny and his men wrote about the many burros in Santa Fe, especially the ones loaded with neatly stacked firewood. Some of those burros went with Kearney's army when it went west to fight in California.

Although the Spanish had been in Taos for centuries, and that town was only a few miles south of Colorado's San

Luis Valley, most Spanish and Mexican settlers had not gone further north than Taos because of the hostile activities of Native Americans, especially the Comanche. When the United States won the Mexican-American War, Mexican settlers felt much safer and started moving into the San Luis Valley. In 1852 Fort Massachusetts was established in the valley as the first military post in today's Colorado, making U. S. soldiers available to help protect settlers from the Native Americans. The fort was moved from its original location to Ft. Garland in 1858, as the first location was hard to defend because of the numerous small hills around it and was also located in a

Because of its strong Spanish heritage, Trinidad (Colorado) had numerous burros and wood-gatherers by 1865.
Courtesy of Denver Public Library Western History Department
(X-1928)

swampy little dell. Many of these early Mexican settlers prospected for gold and silver on a part time basis. Their small discoveries were the basis for a move to the south by many of the Americans of the 1859 Colorado Gold Rush after they found that all the good mining spots had been taken in the northeastern Rockies (then a part of Nebraska Territory). These southern Colorado settlements made the burro readily available to American prospectors.

The burro was plentiful in Colorado in 1859 and 1860 during the Colorado or "Pike's Peak Gold Rush." Burros were generally sold for ten to twenty-five dollars each (depending on the remoteness of the area, the condition and age of the particular animal, and the local supply of burros). It was a good deal at a time when a horse usually brought from twenty-five to one hundred dollars.

Since there is no genetic difference between the Spanish burro and the Eastern donkey, except the burro being a little smaller and a lot scruffier, it was somewhat surprising that the Spanish burros were especially admired by the early Americans in Colorado. The "cute, little fuzzy animals" were often mentioned in guide books, memoirs, and letters sent back home. In fact, easterners who had probably seen hundreds of donkeys still got excited to see a burro.

The burro, although popular with California prospectors, was not as prevalent there as it would become in Colorado, as most of the gold in California was obtained by placer mining that was done by panning streams and dry creek beds for gold flakes and nuggets, which could be kept in a pouch. California prospectors were merely looking for animals to carry their supplies. The hard rock prospector in Colorado of the 1860s needed a burro or a mule; in fact, it was a necessity, not only for carrying supplies when searching for gold, but also for carrying the ore out to the smelters to separate it from worthless rock in which it was found. As thousands of gold hungry prospectors moved towards the Rocky Mountains in 1859 and 1860, they were told in guidebooks and by old-timers (at that point in Colorado history anyone who had prospected for more than a few months) that they *must* have a burro or a mule — and if going very far into the mountains, the burro was preferable.

CHAPTER THREE

The Burro and the Prospector

An Unlikely Friendship in the Old West

The burro was not in widespread use among Anglos within the territory that is now the western United States until it was found to be particularly useful to American prospectors in the mountainous and desert terrain of the Southwest. When gold was discovered in late 1848 in what would later become the State of California, thousands of men made their way to that area, usually arriving on ships. There, many of the prospectors found the lowly burro waiting to take them inland to the gold fields. The burro was not very quick, but was dependable and relatively inexpensive. The animals were being bought from the local Spanish settlers who either had bred them or rounded up feral burros. Many of the gold-seeking California prospectors were Mexican nationals and had brought their own burros with them. The burro became so closely associated with prospecting that when a burro was seen with a full pack of supplies on its back, together with a man on foot, it was instantly known that the owner was a prospector.

In 1859 Colorado prospectors came overland from the eastern United States using many different modes of transportation, including traveling on foot. Wagons and carts were usually pulled by donkeys, mules, and oxen; but some men pulled the carts themselves. A favorite mix of this latter form of transportation was a four-man team — two men pulling the cart, while the other two rested while walking alongside. From 1858 to 1860 prospectors flooded into Colorado — an estimated 50,000 to 100,000 in just two years. Most of these men were looking only for gold nuggets like those found in California ten years earlier. Many quickly went home disappointed, others became miners, and a few kept on prospecting, filled with the eternal hope of striking it rich.

The use of burros started out slowly in Colorado. It was mainly mules brought from back East that were the pack animals of 1859 and 1860. The diaries of the "Pikes Peakers" or "59ers" do not mention the burro often. The original discoveries of gold were along the northern Front Range of Colorado and were placer gold, which was found by panning for gold in the streams. Pack animals were really only needed to transport supplies, and the men were close enough to the open prairies that rich, long grass was cut and brought into the mountains for the mules, oxen, and horses. The hay was sold for very large amounts of money. Men cutting hay and freighting it to the mountains, as a whole, did much better financially than most prospectors. Most of the early gold discoveries were close enough to the prairie that short roads and good trails could be built to the new mines, although some of these roads were very harrowing.

By 1860 the placer gold was basically gone, but the prospectors had learned to look for gold in hardrock veins. It took more equipment to get to this gold, and the gold ore was blasted out and hauled to smelters while still locked into a considerable amount of worthless rock. There was also less grass in the mountains and nothing but narrow Indian trails on which to travel. Given these conditions, the burro was exactly what was needed. As new prospectors moved into the interior of the steep and rugged mountains, it was almost always suggested by those already there that they buy a surefooted and trustworthy burro.

The early Colorado prospectors tended to cluster together for protection from the Native Americans, especially during the War Between the States that started in 1861. During that time, most mining ceased in Colorado as men went back to the East to fight. These men included virtually all of the Union soldiers who would otherwise have been available to safeguard prospectors against hostile Native Americans. The people of Colorado were forced to depend mainly on State militia or informal groups of men for their protection during this time.

Hundreds of thousands of mules, donkeys, and horses were killed during the Civil War, thereby leaving a shortage of these animals — especially for people coming to Colorado from the

This 1860 drawing of Gregory Gulch shows very early Colorado prospectors and their burros and oxen.
Frank Leslie's Illustrated Newspaper, Author's Collection

East. As American prospectors slowly started to come back to look for gold in Colorado, they penetrated deeper and spread out over the mountains. If they had not already heard of them, they soon discovered dependable little burros, especially in the southern part of Colorado Territory, where the animals had already lived for decades.

After the Civil War, the use of the burro, and therefore the number of burros, began to quickly grow. Neither Colorado, nor almost anywhere else in the interior of the West, could have been settled nearly as quickly as it was, if it were not for the burro. When a mining district or a mountain town was young, pack trains of mules and burros were basically the only source of transportation in the rugged mountains; and the burro was better suited than the mule when following steep and narrow Indian trails or when there was no trail at all.

Therefore in a new mining district, burros usually brought the first prospectors, carried their initial tents and supplies, hauled in the materials needed for the first buildings in a new town, and perhaps were used by the first ministers and prostitutes. According to legends, ministers seemed to always arrive in a newly-established town holding on to the tail of their burros in the middle of a blinding snowstorm; while the prostitutes preferred to dress up and drive around town in a buggy to show off the new merchandise that was available.

Alex Carey wrote:

> *The little animals (burros) could, as they desired, be intelligent and stupid, willing but often stubborn, mischievous or docile. They were cussed, discussed, and loved by all. In the opening and operation of the mines in the San Juan region they were indispensible, carrying huge loads over precarious mountain trails, up the steepest hills, around cliffs where hardly a man could walk. They were nearly as sure-footed as a mountain goat.*

In the 1870s, a lot of mining attention turned to silver and lode mining and centered around the San Juans, Sangre de Cristos, and the area between what would become Leadville and Fairplay. All these places were soon full of burros. In the San Juans and Sangre de Cristos, prospectors often came into the mountains from the south from Abiqui, Tierra Amarillo, or Taos, New Mexico. These were "jumping off points" along the Old Spanish Trail, which allowed access to all the mining areas in the southern half of Colorado and was only a stone's throw over Poncha Pass to South Park or the Arkansas River, which could easily be followed up to California Gulch, Fairplay, and the mines in those areas. Supplies coming from the south were generally carried on the backs of burros, and the little creature's name started to pop up regularly in written accounts of the time.

Soon there were towns or supply points all over the San Luis Valley and up the Rio Grande River to Stony Pass and the new settlement of Silverton. Famous pioneer photographer W. H. Jackson, who was with the Hayden Survey, noted as he went over Stony Pass that there were lots of burros and "lots of smashed up wagons there." A little later Ernest Ingersol, one of his companions on the Hayden Survey, wrote:

> *Goods and merchandise of every kind were brought in on the backs of the tough and patient little Mexican burro, toiling along the terrible heights under burdens almost as bulky as themselves.*

Stony Pass was high, steep, and covered with snow for most of the year. Usually the top portion was traversed in early morning when the snow was frozen. Men often had to dig or pack a trail for the short-legged burros. This was done either on foot using shovels or with horses. One novel approach to crossing Stony was reported in the *San Juan Prospector* (a Del Norte newspaper) on March 28, 1874. Burros were being flipped on their side or back and then drug through the snow by the ears.

William Henry Jackson of the Hayden Survey shot this photo of an early milkman (probably burro's milk) peddling in Baker's Park in 1873. The milk was poured from the keg into the small pitcher.
The Burro Book, Author's Collection

This action is a little hard to believe, unless perhaps the animals were totally exhausted from the climb and did not fight back.

Prospectors and their burros also went over Cochetopa Pass and down the Gunnison River. Then those men in search of riches spread out like a fan, following rivers and creeks into the nearby mountains to camps like Crested Butte, Tin Cup, and Ouray. There was no stopping this flood of hopeful humanity, and the burro was right there in the middle of it.

The reason the burro was usually preferred to a mule or a horse was given by one unnamed prospector who said, "The burro could go where the horse cannot, could eat what the mule will not, and when there was nothing to eat, he goes hungry without complaint." Another man put it another way, "A burro doesn't let you mess up as much as a horse will." Yet another wrote, "The horse has never been created that could sustain the hardships of these mountain and desert journeys; and the mule would have died of wrath and discouragement before the prospector got out of sight of his base of supplies."

As author Ken Reyher wrote:

> The diminutive burro stood at the apex of (the) transportation system and continued to hold that position for more than a generation.... They were short, stocky, paunch-bellied, shaggy, and lacked grace and any semblance of equestrian beauty. But whatever cosmetic shortcomings these creatures had were more than made up in their ability to adapt as beasts of burden.

Author Marshall Sprague wrote of similar feelings held by Winfield Stratton, who searched for gold and silver for seventeen years in Colorado with a tough and dependable burro as his constant companion. Stratton went all over the state, following up on new strikes at South Park, Chalk Creek, Baker's Park, Ouray, Leadville, Kokomo, the Wet Mountains, the Elk Mountains, Red Cliff, and Aspen. But for years he was a little too late; a little too unlucky. In the winter he worked as a carpenter to make more money to prospect. Sprague wrote:

> Hunting for mines suited his temperament. Here was the sort of career he wanted. It gave him excitement without the headaches which line the path of ordinary ambition. He enjoyed the aloofness of mountain scenery, the tinkling sound water made up there, the simple way that everything was put together. He liked traveling around with a burro for a companion. Burros did not talk back, quibble, complain, belittle, overcharge, boast or make unreasonable demands. They just did what they were told.

Perhaps another reason prospectors liked the burro was the old European folklore that if a burro's bray was the first sound a person heard in the morning, they could make a wish and it would come true. There is absolutely no doubt that a lot of luck was involved with prospecting, and there was a general feeling among many men that the right burro might bring a man luck. It did not matter what your education was, or the time you had spent prospecting, or the amount of studying you had done. The saying was, "Gold is where you find it, not where it ought to be." Maybe Stratton found out about the tale during his seventeenth year of prospecting and made his wish, because he finally struck it fabulously rich at Cripple Creek.

Even the old timer prospectors believed in good luck or "fate." Otis Young, in his book *Western Mining*, reports that some prospectors used what he called "burro dowsing" to strike it rich. This dowsing was based on the assumption that a burro

The Ute Indians didn't want American prospectors or their burros in the San Juans before they ceded the area in 1873.
Harper's Weekly, October 25, 1879 Author's Collection

could find gold. There were usually two signs that the burro would give — either it would paw the ground at a rich vein or it would make the prospector mad, causing him to pick up a rock to throw at his "stubborn" animal, discovering that the rock was very heavy for its size or had color that was worth investigating. Young also reported that:

> *The presumed ability of jackasses to find mineralization was as much (believed) in Anglo circles as were the prospecting talents of ghosts in Hispanic quarters.*

In addition to the true stories involving burro dowsing and its successful outcome, there are also other stories about prospectors out looking for their burros that had wandered off a ways, thereby causing the prospector to make a rich discovery during the search. Sometimes it is hard to decide whether these stories are fact or fiction, but as they say — "gold is where you find it, not where it ought to be."

The prospector who used the burro was himself very unique and special. Frank Waters described the prospector's mentality in *Midas of the Rockies*. Waters claims that Stratton's seventeen years of frustration "shrank him into a prospector with all of Colorado his home." He went on to explain:

> *They have been battered by the elements and reduced by immense solitudes into an unvarying drabness. Plodding, taciturn men, they all wear the same battered felt hat, the same dirt wool shirts and heavy boots. They speak — when they do speak — in the same guarded voice, they know the same hidden haunts of deer and grouse, are skilled alike in the long-forgotten wilderness arts.... They have gone blithely but slowly, keeping one wary eye for a piece of float, the smallest speck of color.... Of a strange and incomprehensible breed of men to whom*

ON THE BACKS OF BURROS

nothing, neither success, failure, riches nor fame, means anything compared to his never ending search....

Arthur Lakes in *Prospecting for Gold and Silver* wrote that a good prospector was "a miner who became too restless to stick to steady work." A "prospector" should never be confused with a "miner." The miner worked in the mines for a daily pay of about $3.50. The prospector worked only for himself (unless perhaps he had been grubstaked), made no wages, and was free to travel and look for gold and silver wherever he wished. If he had been grubstaked (given money for his supplies by another person — usually enough for one month), he would have to split his discovery at the usual rate of a one-quarter to one-half interest with the man who made the grubstake. Even then, the prospector was still his own man — free to go where and when he wanted. H.A.W. Tabor, Leadville multi-millionaire, was actually a grocery merchant who became fabulously rich by grubstaking prospectors. August Roche and George Hook, men who were grubstaked by Tabor, hit it big with their Little Pittsburg Mine and started Tabor on his way.

The burro was used not only to carry the prospector's tools (shovel, gold pan, pick, and hammer), but also his food (usually flour, bacon, coffee, and sugar) and other supplies like a bedroll, tent, and clothes. If the prospector was especially thoughtful, oats for the burro were also carried on its back for special occasions. *William's Tourist Guide and Map of the San Juan Mines of Colorado* gave an even more detailed suggested list of the "Miner's Outfit." It included $300 to $500 cash, coffee pot, frying pan, camp knife, bake oven, bread pan, three tin plates, knife and fork, coffee mill, tin cup, two teaspoons, two tablespoons, three double blankets, a poncho, a suit of clothes, heavy hobnailed boots, another pair of "camp shoes," a soft hat, overalls and a shirt. Food items that were suggested included one pound of flour for each day out, one-half pound of beef or one-

58

quarter pound of bacon for each day, and a quantity of dried fruit. Suggested tools included drills in several lengths, a six pound hammer and an eight pound hammer, a tracing pick, prospecting pole, long handled shovel, gads, powder, and fuse. Even the burro that had to carry all the equipment and supplies was recommended in William's guide book, which noted: "a good burro will cost about thirty dollars in the San Juan Mining District." Items that were not mentioned by Williams, but which were absolutely necessary, were a canteen or two for water and a jug or two of whiskey for those lonely nights around the campfire.

G. Thomas Ingham, in his book *Digging Gold Among the Rockies*, had this advice to give:

> *Those who expect to prospect should, in some town as near their destination as possible, buy a burro (the Mexican name for a donkey; name used in California and Colorado), which will cost about twenty-five dollars; pack upon his back a supply of provisions, an axe, pick, shovel, cooking utensils, tent and blankets. Drive the animal to any point you choose, and to transport yourself, walk. It costs but a trifle to keep a burro; he will live chiefly upon the pasture along the way, and they are of great assistance in moving from place to place; and are remarkably sure-footed, and will climb the most rugged mountains where other animals would fail. There are thousands of them in use in the Rockies as pack animals. Such an outfit, including the jack and tools, with a month's provisions for two persons, will probably not exceed in costs sixty dollars.*

Most, but not all, of the Colorado prospectors who headed into the rough, high mountains had no previous prospecting experience and realized they needed the advice of experienced men or the local guidebooks, even though many of them had read or been falsely told that the gold was just lying on the

Prospectors were always ready to pose with their burros. These men were at Pitkin, Colorado about 1885.
Photographer Olark's Studio, Denver Public Library
Western History Department (X-60950)

ground, waiting to be picked up. These men were generally called "greenhorn prospectors" as opposed to "professional prospectors," who in Colorado's early mining days usually came from prospecting previously in Georgia or California.

In case a greenhorn prospector still wanted to go searching for gold or silver in the late 1870s, Ingham had four suggestions:

1) *Have a companion or two with you. It is cheaper and safer,*
2) *Take little, travel as light as possible,*
3) *Be ready to walk a lot, and*
4) *Buy a burro.*

Greenhorns were not usually self-sufficient, and they relied mainly on luck to "strike it rich." Their goal was to make a lot of money as quickly and easily as possible. Greenhorn prospectors were often found in town or at the mining camps, trying to find someone to tell them how and where to get rich (as if someone would have actually given them that information). Most of these men gave up quickly and went home. In fact, in the early 1860s, thousands of men left and went home within a few months of arriving in Colorado.

However, some men did not easily get discouraged and quit. They usually read the guidebooks or listened to other men who knew at least something about prospecting. Some went to mining schools to learn geology and assaying. Most of these men learned about prospecting the hard way — by experience. They were usually told to look for "confused" or co-mingled rock that was distinct in color and texture from the surrounding barren rock (called "country rock"). Another good sign was quartz. It seemed that quartz was many times found in abundance around a highly mineralized area. When a mineral vein was harder than the surrounding rock, it would usually show up as white, maroon, or rusty brown outcrops. If the vein was softer than the surrounding rock, it might show up as a trench, notch, depression, or a sudden change in slope.

If the color of softer ores were brown to yellow, it normally meant that iron was present; green or blue colors indicated copper; and black usually meant manganese or lead. Gold was generally associated with iron (except iron pyrite, which was called "fool's gold," but which on occasion might contain gold). Copper was usually associated with silver. Almost any intense color except metallic fool's gold or lemon yellow uranium was worth investigating very closely. If none of the colors were present, the prospector might still pan in a creek or stream or even a dry stream bed. When small gold flakes ("float") were found, he would try to follow this "trace gold" back upstream or uphill to the source, which was usually a vein). But the old axiom also held true — "gold is where you find it, not where it ought to be."

By the end of the 1860s, most of the "strike it rich" green-horn prospectors of the Pikes Peak Gold Rush, or the men who came just after the Civil War, had gone home. By 1880, G. Thomas Ingham wrote in *Digging Gold Among the Rockies*:

> *It can almost be said that prospecting has become a trade or profession. There are men who have followed it a lifetime, and who make it the business of their lives....A few of these own their own property and have comfortable homes and families in the east and elsewhere....yet every summer finds them in the mountains. It is a life they cannot quit, and has a power over them they cannot resist. They are experienced gold hunters.*

There was just one thing Ingham left out — their burros were probably with them and were just as hooked on this way of life as the prospectors were. These were the men who had stayed, patiently prospecting with their burros, year after year, in the rugged mountains of Colorado. These are the men whom history quite correctly remembers.

The stated goal of all prospectors was to make a lot of money; however, for many men the way of life was just as important. Finding a rich discovery was still the goal, but developing a mine to "prove it up" and, if successful, make it worth a lot more money was secondary. Prospectors would often sell out quickly for a relatively small sum when they could have developed their mine just a little more and made five or ten times as much money. But this was not what was important to many of them. They were usually anxious to move on to see what lay over the next mountain or in the next valley and try to make their next big discovery. It was actually a pretty good life, although it had its hardships; and it was a life that a burro fit into perfectly. There were hills, gullies, and mountains in thousands of new places to explore (burros are very inquisitive just like most men). The prospector in Colorado had an extra benefit, as they were living and working in some of the most beautiful places in the world.

The professional prospector came to know the secrets of the mountains well. He traveled lightly and much of the time lived off the land, supplemented by only a few basic supplies. He drifted in and out of the local mining districts, depending on the predominant rumors of the time. Unlike the greenhorns, these prospectors were seldom seen in town — they were almost always out in the mountains. Some of the men searched for decades. Most did not have the money to develop a mine if they did strike a good prospect. At best they would work their claim to the point where they could get a patent (or full legal title to the land). Selling

Prospectors usually made a trail ahead of their burros in deep snow, but sometimes the burro led the prospector, who was hanging onto its tail (the practice was called "tailing".)
Harper's Weekly, June 9, 1883,
Author's Collection

the mine quickly gave the prospector instant profit, no further financial risk, and the ability to move on. It was just what they wanted; and it is mainly to these men that we owe a debt for finding most of the really big and rich strikes in Colorado.

Marshall Sprague did a marvelously accurate job of describing professional prospector in Colorado in the 1870s and 1880s:

> They shaved rarely, wore ancient felt hats, chewed tobacco, drank quantities of whiskey and lived mainly on beans and hope. They were an uneducated, hermit-like breed guided more by superstition than science. That is why everything worth finding was found by them, instead of by the mining engineers who held them in such scorn. Gold is where you find it, not where it ought to be.

If, like a very few and very lucky men, the prospector really did "strike it rich," he might get $50,000 (worth a million dollars today) or more for his basically unproven claim and would be set for life. But many of these men still continued to prospect, even after marrying, building a beautiful new home, and having a family. A small discovery might bring in only a few thousand dollars, but it was enough money to resupply and keep looking for the big strike for a few more years. Prospecting got under a man's skin, kind of like gambling does for some people today. It was the search that brought the most excitement, not the pot of gold at the end of the prospector's rainbow. A man could be easily hooked on this kind of life, and his faithful burro usually played a very important part in it.

When winter came to the high mountains, the prospectors and their burros usually went to lower country, where they might or might not continue prospecting. Some men just "hung around" for the winter, letting their burros eat whatever they could find. Others would get a part-time job; or, if they had

Prospectors usually went to lower altitudes in the winter. These men are packing their burros in the spring to head back into the mountains.

Harper's Weekly, November 10, 1888, Author's Collection

made a good discovery and had some money tucked away, they often lived with their families in a nice home. But one thing was for certain — they and their burros would be headed back to the high country in the spring.

Besides the burro carrying all the food and supplies while it and its master were traveling, once the prospector and his burro set up camp, the burro still had plenty of work to do. It carried coal or firewood, acted as a burglar alarm, served as a companion, and accomplished many other tasks. Sometimes the burro would pull the prospector's pick through the ground like a plow to loosen up the dirt for panning. If a discovery was made, the burro might work a crude arrastra to crush the ore, haul water for panning dirt, or conversely, haul dirt to water where it could be panned.

When a claim was first staked, it was an "unpatented claim." The prospector who held this type claim did not yet have full legal title to the property. "Assessment work" had to be done every year for at least five consecutive years on an unpatented claim. Only then could a prospector apply, pay a small fee for a patented claim, and have full legal title. Assessment work included such things as building a cabin or digging a shaft. A burro was always indispensible with this type of work. And, of course, if good ore was found, the burro was used to carry it back to civilization to be assayed or milled.

The burro's sociable nature especially appealed to prospectors who might be in the mountains by themselves for months at a time. Often this special relationship between the burro and the prospector was shared with another four-legged creature — the dog. Although not all dogs and burros got along well, many of them were very close friends because they have very similar personalities. Given his life of solitude, the prospector and his animals often became very attached, as can be seen in the fact that almost all prospectors named their animals and talked to them. Burros' names were as numerous and as imaginative as the names of the claims that the prospectors staked. Some burro names were based on the prospector's old girl friends, wife, or mother; while others were based on the burro's personality traits or color. Names like Blue, Bummer, Floppy, Shorty, Sweetie, and Plain Jane are just a few examples, and all are very descriptive. When back in civilization for supplies, many prospectors had their photo taken with their burros, so that they could remember their buddies later, or send photographs home to their relatives so they could see their new friends.

John Cowan tried to explain this special relationship between the prospector and his burro when he wrote:

> The burro is the companion, friend, and half-brother
> of the prospector; the sharer of his tales and hardship,
> the partner of his joys, the helper in his success, the
> equal sufferer of his failures.

Burros were sometimes taken into dance halls or saloons by their owners, and most of the time no one got upset. In fact, the burro often had its photograph taken with all the men at the bar. After all, the little creatures had probably hauled the liquor to the saloon and the musical instruments to the dance hall, so why not? Groups of burros were often reportedly seen at the doors and windows of saloons and dance halls, listening to the music (although it has been shown that burros prefer classical music), intently watching the commotion that was going on inside, and obviously having a good time themselves.

One of the best efforts at capturing the very special relationship between a prospector and his burro (in this case her name was the unimaginative "Jenet") is included in Zane Grey's book, *Tappan's Burro*. To quote Grey:

> *Tappan, in common with most lonely wanderers of the desert, talked to his burro. As the years passed this habit grew, until Tappan would talk to Jenet, just to hear the sound of his voice. Perhaps that was all that kept him human.*

(Burros actually enjoy being talked to very much, whether or not they actually understand what is being said. They just enjoy the attention.) Tappan and his burro shared many hardships, which created great trust between them. Unfortunately Tappan broke this trust, but in the end had a chance to redeem himself. When it was suggested that he abandon Jenet, he replied:

> *I can't go on without her. It'd never entered my head. Jenet's mother was a good, faithful burro. I saw Jenet born way down there on the Rio Colorado. She wasn't strong. An' I had to wait for her to be able to walk.... How many times in ten years Jenet has done me a good turn I can't remember. But she saved my life.*

Yes, the burro held a very special place in the hearts of many prospectors. It was a true friend that never deserted its master, no matter how rough the going got (although it might hide for a while — just for the fun of it). Many prospectors were able to train their burros to follow them without a rope, much like a dog will follow its master. Many burros ate the left over or spoiled food of their masters, and since the prospector ate mainly beans, pancakes and bacon, those foods usually became the favorite meal of his burro.

Unlike the horse, burros did not usually wander very far away from camp at night, even without hobbles. In fact there were many tales of burros regularly waking their masters early in the morning, anxious to get their breakfast. Most prospectors did not mind this a bit. The prospectors would often let their burros stay inside their cabins in the winter — not just to keep the animals warm, but also for companionship. A prospector had faith and trust in his burro to take care of him, and the burro had the same faith and loyalty to a good master. Burros are always quick to return the love and kindness shown to them by humans.

There are literally thousands of tales that were told about individual Colorado prospectors, their burros, and their quests for gold and silver. There are hundreds of these tales that have been written down and are still known today. We only have space for a few specific stories, but they are well worth retelling.

William Harvey came to Colorado, changed his name to Nicholas Creede (no one knows for sure why, and searched the Rockies from Canada to Mexico for many years with only a burro and a dog that he named "Whiskers" as companions. We do not know the burro's name, which seems to show a little favoritism. Creede was actually pretty successful but plowed most of his money back into prospecting. He finally struck it rich in 1890 at his "Holy Moses Mine" near present-day Creede, Colorado. Creede discovered the famous mine fairly late in Colorado mining history. It is said that he named the mine because when he saw the rich ore he said, "Holy Moses, I have struck it rich!" The discovery supposedly came about while Creede was trying to drive a stake into the ground to secure his burro.

You would think that Creede would have taken better care of his burro, since he also became the owner of another famous mine in the area due to the actions of burros. A prospector friend named Renniger was trying to catch three of his burros. They were staying just outside his reach, and he was unsuccessful in getting them to go back to camp. Sprague wrote:

> *He sat down to await their pleasure. Sitting, he began a casual chipping on a nearby ridge which showed mineral in such quantity that he thought he had better seek more experienced advice and brought Creede to see it. Creede looked at it and begged Renninger to define the claim at once. Renninger, offering thanks up to the three donkeys, did so and they named it the Last Chance. Then Creede located next to his property, shoulder to shoulder, and named his claim the Amethyst. These became two of the fabulously rich mines in Creede fame. All from the contrariness of three burros.*

Most people have heard the famous poem written by Cy Warman, editor of the *Creede Chronicle*, about "It's day all day in the daytime, and there is no night in Creede." However few recognize that the burro rightly has a part in the whole stanza:

> *Here's a land where all are equal—*
> *Of high and lowly birth—*
> *A land where men make millions,*
> *Dug from the dreary earth.*
> *Here the meek and mild-eyed burros*
> *On mineral mountains feed,*
> *It's day all day in daytime,*
> *And there is no night in Creede.*

Creede sold his properties, became rich, let his burro loose to fend for itself, and left for California to retire. Obviously, Creede's motives were not "the way of life" but the "striking it rich" part of the story. He took his dog Whiskers with him but left his burro behind. No one seems to know what happened to Creede's other animal "partner."

Winfield Scott Stratton was another example of one of those men who prospected for a long time with his burro. Most of this time was spent in the Colorado mountains. Eventually, his clothes were torn and ragged, and his burro was thin, sick, and footsore. Stratton's bad luck is described by author Frank Waters in his book *Midas of the Rockies* as being "as persistent as the burro at his heels," but he finally struck it big at Cripple Creek, right in the middle of ranching country, a place that just did not look right for prospecting.

Stratton had come close to striking it rich several times. Back in 1885, he was prospecting in Imogene Basin near Ouray. The area had been worked for a decade, with only small amounts of silver being found. The man who originally discovered the basin was a prospector named Andy Richardson, who lived in Imogene Basin for years, all the time thinking he would strike it rich at any time. He found ore, but it was so low grade that it was not be worth shipping to the mills or smelters. Stratton had the same experience. What neither of them knew was that the area was very rich in tellurium gold, which was not visible to the naked eye. Less than ten years later, Andy Richardson took a man to the basin in the hope of selling him some of his "average" silver discoveries. Tom Walsh had taken assaying classes, did an assay of the ore, and discovered the gold. The discovery made Walsh one of the richest men in the world. "Gold is where you find it, not where it ought to be."

Stratton later took assaying classes himself and used his knowledge to discover the fabulously rich Cripple Creek Mining District. While packing his burro to go on his life changing prospecting trip to the Cripple Creek area, his burro kept throwing its pack off because of the painful aggravation of a major wound that the burro had received during a tangle with some barbed wire. Stratton got frustrated, especially after bystanders started laughing. He took a swing at the burro with a board, knocked the scab off the wound, and the burro started bleeding profusely. A woman who witnessed this event told him she was leaving to call the authorities to report him for animal abuse (a rarity where burros were concerned), but Stratton took a hasty retreat out of town and just days later made the big discovery that changed his life forever. Gold — in a cow pasture? Well, "Gold is where you find it, not where it is supposed to be."

A much more typical case was that of A.W. "Gus" Begole, who was running a mining supply store at Ouray in the San Juan Mountains in southwest Colorado at about the same time that the luckless Stratton was there. Begole and Stratton became friends, and Begole may have even grubstaked Stratton. Begole and his burro had been in the San Juans with the first American prospectors in 1860, and he was back in the San Juans with his burro in the early 1870s, when prospecting picked up again after the Civil War. He and his burro were there in 1875 when Begole and other men first came into the valley that holds today's little town of Ouray, Colorado. Begole and John Eckles discovered several mines in the area, including the Mineral Farm Mine, which was very unusual as its mineral veins ran on top of the surface. This allowed the extent of the veins to be easily perceived, and many of the veins could be mined by digging trenches, much like a farmer might dig potatoes. Hence the name — "The Mineral Farm Mine."

Even though the mine would have been an easy one for Begole and Eckles to develop, just a year after the discovery they sold it for $75,000 cash (Begole demanded that the purchase price be paid in greenbacks on the spot). That sum was a large amount of money in those days, but the mine eventually made over a million dollars profit. Begole, who was getting too old to continue to prospect, opened a miner's supply store in Ouray and started grubstaking other prospectors. He was not rich, but he was prosperous. Supposedly Begole's burro spent the rest of his life in town, just taking it easy with his friend "Gus."

The difference between striking it rich and never doing very well was a very slim one in Colorado's mountains. Chance played a very big part in prospecting; the burro did too. If it did not bring its master luck (or actually show him where the ore was), most prospectors still realized that some things are more valuable than monetary riches — God, family, and friends — even friends with fuzzy heads and very long, furry ears.

Sometimes their sociable nature would get burros in trouble, especially when they were in town for a while. Towns were just not made for burros or professional prospectors. Judge Moses Hallet, on his first trip to visit Silverton, stayed at the Grand Imperial Hotel at the center of town, yet reported that the burros and mules in the corrals started braying at two in the morning and did not stop until four, when the cooks at the hotel took over making noise while preparing breakfast. The burros' noise got so bad in Fairplay and Cripple Creek that some citizens wanted them banned from those towns at night.

At times that sociable nature would cause problems even far away from a town. When gold and silver were discovered at Burrows Park, many prospectors rushed to the spot with their furry friends. The local newspaper reported that so many burros were braying at night when there was a full moon that the stage passengers trying to sleep at the local stage stop were complaining that they could not get any rest.

All of the prospecting in Colorado was not done by men traveling alone. Some prospectors preferred to travel in groups, but there were still usually burros with them. With the one-on-one companionship gone, the burros and the prospectors did not have such a close relationship, but they still enjoyed each others' company. Prospectors traveling in groups (usually three to eight men) would quite often have a few more burros than one for each man, in order to carry tents, extra tools, and other supplies or equipment they felt to be important. Usually there was an agreement that if a discovery was made by anyone in the group, it would be shared with the other men.

Whether single or in a group, the burro was a true friend of the prospector — it never deserted, usually forgave, and sometimes even saved the life of its human friend. Some burros were even buried beside their masters or vice versa. Regardless of where a prospector's burro was buried, the burial was usually done with the same reverence its master would have given a deceased human friend.

Because a burro seemed to usually be around at the time of a big mining discovery, when a prospector died without revealing

A prospectors' camp on Alder Creek, San Miguel County, Colorado about 1880 included plenty of burros and a few horses.
Photo by Clark Studio, Courtesy of Denver Public Library
Western History Department (X-60900)

the location of his rich mine, there was always a fleeting hope in other prospectors' minds that his burro might take them to the location. Tales of lost gold mines exist all over Colorado and the West, but the following is a tale of a lost gold mine and burros that happened in the San Juan Mountains.

Levi Carson came into Silverton one day in 1890 with a type of ore that was not like any seen before in the area. Two hundred pounds of the ore sold for $2,400 (about $100,000 at today's prices.). Carson walked into town with his burros from the south, from up by Coal Bank Hill and Molas Pass, an area that had experienced a horrific forest fire about a decade before. It took Carson and his burros several days to get through this area because of all the tangled, fallen dead trees, and it was easy to lose anyone who tried to follow them. Nevertheless, several men found out enough to suspect that Levi was going into the nearby West Needle Mountains. Carson came back to Silverton several more times with his burros fully loaded with rich ore, and he always turned down offers to buy his mine. On one return trip to his mine, Carson had a heart attack and died on Molas Pass, where his body and his burros (alive and well) were found by travelers.

On many occasions men have tried to find the "Lost Carson Mine." They did succeed in finding a camp with a corral and other provisions for Carson's burros, but Carson had told a relative that the mountain was too steep to take even the burros to the mine, so he had to bring the ore down himself before the burros could pack it out to Silverton. To this day the rich mine has never been found, despite the efforts of several treasure hunters.

Many stories have been told of burros saving their masters from imminent dangers or providing companionship, comfort and solace in the dangerous and lonesome wilderness of Colorado. Rev. J. J. Gibbons wrote of a prospector whose burro warned him of an upcoming flash flood in the small gulch in which they were camped for the night. The burro ran up to the tent and brayed until his master woke up, came out, and saw just how fast the water was rising in the nearby creek. The burro's keen sense of smell and hearing was often helpful, when he brought his owner to drinking water, or warned his master of approaching bandits.

There are tales of burros carrying injured masters, unconscious, on their backs for medical help. Burros have saved their owners from attacks by bears and wolves, and, sometimes before an attack could happen, they have warned their masters of danger ahead of time. And then there are tales of prospectors who risked their lives to save their burros, usually in icy streams.

Levette Davis in "Rocky Mountain Burro Tales" tells of a prospector who broke his leg very seriously and could not move. There was no way he was going to be able to climb on his burro's back, so he tied a note requesting help to his burro's tail, and sent the animal to town. The burro delivered the message, and the prospector's life was saved.

Not all of these stories were life and death matters or even involved the prospectors themselves. Augusta Tabor (H.A.W. Tabor's wife) came to Denver, Colorado, with her husband in 1859. The Tabors moved with their young child into South Park and then to the Arkansas River Valley in the area that would eventually become Leadville, where they lived in tents in the deep snow and extreme cold of February, 1860. It was the worst time of the winter and so cold that Augusta wrote of a wandering burro, which, in an attempt to keep warm, came to their tent and stood in the campfire they had going just outside. The fire singed the burro's hair near its hooves, but the burro was not seriously hurt. The burro's owner could not be found, so it became the transportation for Augusta and her baby for the rest of the trip. The same burro later came to her tent, went inside and laid down. (And who says burros are stupid!) Augusta had been at the camp by herself for many days and laid her head on the burro's back and "cried with loneliness." Later the jack carried Augusta and her baby across the Arkansas River without a problem, "although he could only keep his nose above water."

In addition to prospecting and transportation, burros were often used to power machinery at the mines, such as arrastras, windlasses, and ore cars. Arrastras were circular pits with a very hard and smooth floor, and a low wall around the outside edge of the circle. From an upright pole in the middle hung a horizontal log that had dangling ropes that led to large, hard rocks that weighed 150 to 200 pounds each. The rocks were dragged on the ground around the circle by the burro, which was attached to the other (outer) end of the horizontal bar. The hard rocks were suspended so that they "nipped" the ore. Eventually the large rocks would pulverize the ore that had been placed in the depression, and the operators would take the pulverized rock and pan it for gold.

This system was terribly inefficient, usually recovering less than half the gold, and was very hard on the burros as well. They were usually blindfolded during their work and sometimes were

A recreated arrastra shows how the device worked, although the burro is not harnessed to the arm.
Denver Public Library Western History Department (X-60014)

This photo was taken about 1890 near Ouray by William Henry Jackson and shows how the burros ran loose but the horses were kept in shelters.
Denver Public Library Western History Department (WHJ-10165)

walked for hours upon end, day after day. Unfortunately for the burros, the arrastra was all that was available at most new discoveries. Sometimes there were tons of rock to be crushed that contained only a few ounces of gold.

Burros were also used on winches, which were cylinders upon which rope or cable was wrapped to pull an ore bucket out of a shaft. Sometimes the miners rode in these buckets, trusting their very lives to the burro that was letting them down or pulling them up. This was especially dangerous work for the burro and the men, as the cable could snap, sending everyone and everything in all directions. A snapped or loose cable could cut a man or an animal in half.

The ore cars initially used at Colorado mines were small, usually holding only about a half ton of ore. At a new mine, a burro might pull one or two of these cars with a half-ton load of ore in each. In the later development of the mine, a burro might be hooked to several cars that could hold one ton of rock each. If the animal had to be taken down a shaft to get to the ore cars, it was usually left there, often never seeing daylight again. Burros were fed and watered underground, and, if lucky, might have a small stall somewhere in the mine.

Quite often the mines in Colorado were forced to temporarily shut down in the dead of winter because of snow. Most miners or prospectors did not take their burros with them when leaving by stagecoach or train for the winter. The burros were usually released near town and were expected to forage for themselves. The burros were generally able to do okay; and the local children were allowed to ride the burros, if they could catch them. Then in the spring the miners and freighters would round up their animals and start packing to the mines again.

Unfortunately, there came a time in this relationship between man and beast, when the prospector had made his discoveries, sold out, and moved on to other areas. Or perhaps the prospector had grown old, given up, gone home, or, like Levi Carson, even died. The burro almost always stayed behind, as there was usually no place for it where its owner was going. Perhaps the prospector even felt his little friend would be safer and happier if it was free and on its own in the mountains of Colorado. Many burros ended up in the local mining camps, scrounging for whatever food they could find in the garbage dump or being fed by local women and children. Often a family with children might take a burro or two in as pets or to use for transportation. For most burros, however, they were either sold to another prospector, rounded up and put to a variety of uses, or killed.

For a while — just for a few decades — Colorado and the Old West had the prospector and his burros, and their very special way of life. This unique relationship was described in a tongue-in-cheek article in the *Fairplay Flume* in January of 1882, and quoted in Linda Bjorklund's book, *Burros!*:

> *I admire the burro. Not for his wild, roving eye, nor*
> *for his remarkably complete ear, or even his seductive*

voice. *These things are transitory. Beauty is the creature of an instant. The bloom upon the rose leaves
almost as quickly as the bloomer on the rose bush.
The quality which should attract respect and admiration of man are more sterling in their nature.*

*I admire his perseverance. Some people call it
obstinacy, but they take a narrow view of the burro's
character. They look at him through a single-barreled
eyeglass. I have seen a burro work for hours to get his
foot stuck in an empty tomato can, and when he suc-
ceeds I have known him to go miles out of his way in
the darkness of midnight, to wake up some drowsy
prospector with his melancholy tintinnabulation. I
have known him to come back repeatedly with his ser-
enade, although he had not been encored and no floral
offering had been received.*

*It was often a burro that carried the huge landscape camera,
large glass plates, and other photo equipment of the nineteenth
century photographer.*

The Burro Book, Author's Collection

I have seen him crawl under the projecting bed of a railroad wagon and strain every nerve to boost it off the road. True, he did not succeed in his design, but he did everlastingly mash two coffee pots and destroy the continuity of his owner's bedding.

I have seen him desert a bale of hay to go and munch cactus and gravel. He couldn't get the same amount of nourishment from the latter in the same space of time, but he scorned to be influenced by such a consideration.

I respect his digestive apparatus. One day I stood on a mountain side with a dyspeptic from Greeley, who for years had eaten nothing but Graham bread and cracked wheat. We were watching a burro feed. As the animal slowly and conscientiously chewed up the flour and gunny sacks, got away with salt bags and ham covers, gathered in brown paper and old sacks, and finally tackled a large-sized sardine box, the tears welled up in the Greeley man and in a husky voice he said: "Lord, if I could only do that."

I worship the intellect of the burro. He cannot be humbugged. He knows when he is within clubbing distance, and when he is not, you can yell at him till you are black in the face and he won't move. Some of the incidents that attest his sagacity are almost marvelous. I was once sitting on a soft sandstone boulder, in a little mining town of C_____. Down the meandering street came old Skipton, driving before him one of the most remarkable looking jacks I ever saw. In the ruggedness of his physical composition he was almost scenic. Half of his left ear was gone and numerous clear places on his hide made it apparent that he was addicted to the hot bath.

"Where did you get that wreck, Skip?" I asked.

"Wreck," he replied scornfully, "why, you damn tenderfoot, that's Henry Ward Beecher. He's the father of his country and he's just got more brain power than any jack in the state."

"Intellectual, is he?" I inquired.

"Well, I should blush. Why I'll just tell you a little act he did yesterday. We was a working up on the High Hopes, me and Jim Atkinson, my pardner, and we got to feeling a little puckish about noon, and I went up to the shanty to fire up. Well, Jim he was sacking up a few pounds of ore to have sampled, and Henry Ward was a standing by, and somehow Jim he slipped and fell into the shaft, but he caught on the bucket and she commenced a flying-down like thunder, and the shaft was nigh onto a hundred feet deep. Well, what did Beecher do? Why he knew it wouldn't do to try and stop the handle, so he just backed up against the windlass and held hard till he stopped her and saved Jim's life. That's what he did and I'll take my paralyzed oath on it, and so'll Jim. See where it took the skin off his haunches?"

The cuticle was evidently gone and Skip looked most solemnly in earnest. I could not doubt him. We went across the street and Skip took a little ginger in his.

The compassionate and loving burro had managed to embed itself deeply into Colorado's social, cultural, and business history. This little companion became almost mystic and spiritual in its bearing, perhaps because of its overwhelming goodness. Words like "meditative," "tender," "wise," "modest," "noble," "compassionate" and "dignified" were used to describe the little animal. The burro shows up often in Western American poetry, art, philosophy, music, and history; but perhaps most importantly, it found a joyous and tender spot in thousands of human hearts.

CHAPTER FOUR

Ƨ☯ƨ

Used and Abused
Moving the West's Freight

THE BURRO

When Adam named in days of old,
The birds and beasts and every fold,
He gave to each his proper class,
And well defined the gentle ass.

His ears made long, inclined to flap,
Down his shoulders is nature's strap.
Thus marked, he went o'er the world wide,
To help us all by easy stride.

Docile, humble, of low degree,
Destined ever a slave to be,
He took his place when time began,
And since has been the friend of man....

Away on mountain, far from throng,
The sound he made, man called a song.
So, moved by notes, most deem scary,
Some dub him now the new canary.

From early morn to close of day,
He sings his song the same old way.
His voice is harsh, a choking roar,
And fills the mind with thoughts of gore.

His notes, one short, with two quite long,
Contain the burden of his song.
At midnight hour when nature rests,
His crooning bray breaks out the best,
And o'er the crags and passes bleak,
His voice resounds in dismal shriek,
And some will cry when they are airy,
That "he's a bird — a true canary."

The burro is his Spanish name,
And bearing it he rose to fame;
For up and down 'neath driver's wrath,
He climbed with load on narrow path
Where slippery trails and icy slate
Precipitate him to his fate.

Plodding along at break of day,
So year by year he makes his way,
Loaded heavy in mountain dust,
In winter's snows and clouds that burst....

Sometimes limping from saddle sores
Dug in his back by sacks of ore.
Taking ills like a patient man,
He spends his time the best he can,

Careless of wounds and battered feet,
Stumbling along the stony streets;
Or standing meek with load or pack,
Eats the hay from his partner's pack....

His faithfulness should prompt us so
To treat him well where e'er we go.
A friend to all on dreary pass,
Most useful is the modest ass.

Rev. J. J. Gibbons

Transportation has always been a vital part of the mining industry of Colorado. Unlike California, where most prospectors panned for gold nuggets or flakes, Colorado was primarily a "hardrock" mining district. The rich ore was blasted from the rock and then usually had to be transported some distance to mills and smelters to release the gold and silver from the barren rock. For about twenty years (in the early 1860s to early 1880s)

A pack burro train on Ute Pass out of Colorado Springs is identified on different versions of the stereo card as on its way to Leadville or the San Juans.

Photographer R. J. Luesly, Author's Collection

this task was done on the backs of burros and mules until good wagon roads and railroads were finally built, and it continued on a lesser scale well into the twentieth century. Hauling freight and ore by burros and mules was expensive, as tons of ore had to be moved 150 to 350 pounds at a time. Rates for shipping ore to the smelters in Colorado's early mining days could reach as high as $200 per ton, which meant that only the very richest ore would be worth more than the shipping costs alone. A mining prospect had to be accessible to get ore out to recover some of the costs and to get supplies in to the mine. However the mine owner was (and still is) always striving to get his transportation costs as low as possible, in order to make the lower grade ores profitable to ship and hopefully make an overall profit.

There were few public funds available for road building in early Colorado that could have made wagon travel common in the mountainous areas. When roads were built, they were usually toll roads, and the fees for passage over these roads were high. For example, the toll to travel the Million Dollar Highway from the Red Mountain Mining District to the City of Ouray was one dollar per burro for a six mile trip — a charge that today would be close to ten dollars. A wagon paid six dollars, cheaper than the toll for ten burros (which would be needed to carry the same amount of ore), but still very expensive. The little narrow gauge railroads (three feet between the rails) dropped costs substantially, but were not built into most of the mining areas of Colorado until the 1880s and 1890s. Therefore, from 1859 until the 1880s burros and mules carried almost all of the needed equipment and supplies to Colorado's mines and mountain towns and also brought almost all of the ore from the mines down to the mills and smelters.

Even when wagon roads and railroads were built in the 1880s and 1890s, there was still a need for burros in the more remote areas of Colorado, although they were mainly used for short hauls of ten miles or less to get the ore to the railroads. There were also a few small, remote mines that had longer hauls.

Even though mining operations continued in Colorado from 1900 to 1920, big mines were prevalent and they primarily used aerial trams to get their ore to the railroads. This eliminated not only the need for pack mules and burros but also the use of ore wagons.

But for twenty to thirty years the answer to Colorado's transportation problem was usually only the burro. As Ken Reyher wrote in his book *Silver and Sawdust*:

> *The diminutive burro stood at the apex of the San Juan transportation system (as well as most of Colorado) and continued to hold that position for more than a generation. California miners first discovered the versatility of these creatures in 1849, and their use spread across the West in subsequent years.*

The more isolated a mine or the more rugged its surrounding terrain, the more likely that burros would be used as the primary source of transportation for all the items that were needed in the mountains. The animals might be carrying large, heavy, bulky loads like doors, stoves, big timbers, and ore cars. Entire crushing mills were prefabricated in small pieces so that they could be brought through the mountains on the backs of burros, even though the assembled machine weighed thousands of pounds. Burros also carried tons of coal and firewood to run the mine's boilers and for heat.

Duane Vanderbusche, referring to *The Gunnison Review-Press* of July 16, 1887, notes some of the large pack trains that ran between Aspen and Crested Butte before the railroad made it to Aspen:

> *Prior to 1887, when the great silver camp of Aspen was finally reached by the Denver and Rio Grande Railroad, long lines of 400 to 500 jacks could be observed on the tops of East Maroon and Pearl Passes*

bringing silver ore to the nearest railhead at Crested Butte. Gothic was a stop on the East Maroon Trail and "appeared quite lively... when constantly passing pack trains to and from Aspen chance to get here at once.... Jack trains were also used extensively to transport ore from Snowmass City, high up in Lead King Basin on the north fork of Rock Creek, and from such rich mines as the Black Queen near the town of Crystal. The ore had to be shipped by long Jack trains along treacherous Crystal Canyon, past the Devil's Punchbowls and Emerald Lake to Gothic, and finally to Crested Butte...."

Thus the courageous little burro had its day high in the Rockies during the early years of the Gunnison Country. The little animal became legendary for his feats of courage and endurance....Someday the Gunnison country may fittingly erect a memorial to one of its great benefactors — the rugged, much maligned, but faithful burro. With little lineage, like most of the hard-rock miners he served, the trusted little animal saved the day in the rugged and high mountains of the Gunnison country. More than a few isolated mining camps owe their existence to him.

T. A. Rickard wrote that "the patient burro (donkey) will walk over ledges which bring a tremor to the hearts of those that are not a mountaineer." Once a good enough trail existed, both burros and mules carried freight. At this stage of trail and road development, there was still an advantage for the burro in that it was small and it had a shorter turning radius. It could therefore navigate steep, sharp switchbacks that a mule could not handle. The burro could climb steeper slopes than a mule and could more easily go under the limbs of trees hanging over the trail. But its biggest advantage was that it was more sure-footed and less likely to slip on the steep and often wet trails.

*These burros were loaded with mine track and other supplies in
Central City about 1880.*
Photographer Charles Weitfle, Denver Public Library
Western History Department (X-21776)

A problem was usually encountered when a burro came to a
stream or creek. The burro does not like to go into water, even
though it actually crosses a stream pretty well. Presumably its
hesitation comes from not being sure how deep the water is,
what might be under the surface, or how it will keep its footing.
However its fear might be one of long standing — an instinct
inherited from the danger posed by crocodiles that were often in
the waters of the burro's native Africa. One possible solution to
this problem was provided by the Reverend George Darley, who
reported that burros had to have their ears tied up when crossing water or they would drown. Once their ears were tied up, he
claimed they could be pushed in and pulled by a rope across a
stream or river without much danger, even when the water was
much deeper than they were tall. "As soon as his ears are untied,
his voice is loosened and breaks forth in trumpet tones of rejoic-
ing, loud enough to be heard far and near."

One task that Colorado burros took on without much hesitation seems unnatural because of their innate caution, but possible because of their lack of fear of heights or narrow trails. Burro pack trains could pass over a deep chasm on a swinging or very narrow bridge made of only a couple of logs. These types of bridges became known in many places as "burro bridges." There was even a community with this name located at the beginning of the Ophir Pass trail out of Silverton. From 1881 until the Rio Grande Southern Railroad was built to Telluride in 1891, burros and mules transported ore from the Telluride and Rico area mines to be milled in or shipped out of Silverton by way of the Ophir Toll Road. The little community of Burro Bridge (population approximately ten) was at the fork of the Ophir and Red Mountain pack trails and had large stables and corrals for the hundreds of burros that went over either pass. There was a pretty massive system of other businesses that was always needed for this type of transportation. Barns, corrals, blacksmiths, livery stables, and if burros were used in the winter or if mules were used at any time of the year, hay and grain needed to be shipped in and stored.

Burros did not hesitate to go over this narrow burro bridge, which could have been near the settlement of the same name.

Author's Collection

Burros did not just carry supplies and ore for the mines. Most early Colorado mining camps owed their very existence to the burro trains that snaked through the mountains and brought in the furniture, equipment, glass, and other necessities that allowed a true town to be built. Sometimes huge groups of 300 to 500 animals ventured into the more remote settlements and camps with badly needed supplies and materials. Newspaper presses, huge coffee grinders, gambling tables, organs, and thousands of other large, heavy items came in to the mountain communities, bringing civilization on the backs of burros.

Just how much a burro train meant to these isolated communities can be seen in a quote from the May 6, 1876 *La Plata Miner* of Silverton, Colorado:

> *Last Tuesday afternoon our little community was thrown into a state of intense excitement by the arrival of the first train of jacks, as they came into sight about a mile above town. Somebody gave a shout,*

Prospectors pose by their burros in early Cripple Creek about 1890.
Photographer D. P. Morgan, Denver Public Library
Western History Department (61139)

'turn out the jacks are coming," and sure enough there were the patient homely little fellows filing down the trail. Cheer after cheer was given, gladness prevailed all around, and the national flag was run up at the post office. It was a glad sight, after six long weary months of imprisonment, to see the harbinger of better days, to see these messengers of trade and business, showing that once more the road was open to the outside world.

Whether they totaled four or four hundred, burros were normally used in groups for freighting. There were several methods that a freighter might use to get his burros to the desired location. Typically, they were driven from behind by several men on horseback; and like sheep, there was often a highly trained dog or two to keep the burros going the way that was desired. Pack burro trains such as this had a lead burro (which often carried no load) that was trained to keep the group moving in the right direction. Burros require almost no training to move in a group together or to carry a pack on their back. It just comes naturally to them.

The men who drove the burros were called "jack-whackers" or "burro-punchers," and they usually hit the animals with small sticks or whips or had their dogs nip at the burros' heels to keep them moving in the right direction. Burros did not need a trail like a horse or mule. They could go almost anywhere. When freighting, burros were usually expected to make a roundtrip to the mine and back in one day. When heading back to the barn without a load, they would often be let loose, and they would usually make it back home cross-country on their own just fine.

If a group of burros (called a "herd" when not tied together or a "string" or "train" when tied together) was being driven from behind and came to an unfamiliar fork in the road, the freighter would use either verbal commands or a whistle to tell his dog whether he wanted the herd to go left or right. The dog would, in turn, nip at the heels of the lead burro to get it to go the way the freighter wanted it to go. A good burro-herding dog was worth several hundred dollars, but usually would not be sold for any amount of money, as the highly trained dog helped to assure that the owner always had a job.

When traveling in a loose formation, the burros would usually end up in a rough V (with the lead burro at the point of the V), which tended to force traffic coming from the opposite direction off the road. However T. A. Rickard, noted mining engineer around 1900, wrote:

> When burros (the word "donkey" being rarely heard in the mining regions) are engaged in packing, they are not tied together, but each goes loose, and the owner drives them like a flock of sheep, though differing from the later in that they have learned, from the narrowness of the trails, to walk single file when that is required for safety....The burro can eke out a precarious existence on the scant grass of the mountain slopes, and for this reason he has been most serviceable to the pioneer and the prospector; if the camel be named "the ship of the desert," the patient, long-eared friend of the miner might well be christened "the porter of the hills."

The burro does not like to back up, which was a problem when meeting someone on a narrow trail. The burro's hesitation to put itself into reverse seems to come from not knowing where he is going or who or what is behind him. Come to think of it, most humans do not like to back up either. So in this situation there was a danger not only to the burro trains, but also to the travelers they met along the way. If the trail was narrow, and especially in the winter, a traveler might have to swing his feet over the saddle towards the inside of the trail and wait for the

A train of burros is being "encouraged" by burro-whackers as they carry their load of lumber on a trail through deep snow.
Harper's Weekly, June 9, 1883, Author's Collection

burros to pass, or as an alternative back up to find a place where he could get out of the way and allow the burro train to pass. A person in a buggy might have to unharness his team and pull his buggy up the side of the mountain to let a burro train pass.

If there was no dog, there would have to be at least two burro punchers, so one of the men could run or ride ahead of the burros to get them to go the correct way. If only one man was trying to command a group of burros, and he had no dog, he would almost always have to tie the burros together in a line for control purposes. Being tied together was a situation that most burros did not like. It was a real task to keep a large burro train constantly moving, and a really good burro puncher that could do this was worth his weight in the gold or silver that the little animals usually carried. Experienced burro punchers also understood their animals, realized that each one had its own idiosyncrasies, responded accordingly, and rarely mistreated them.

If the burros were to be used while tied together for a burro train, Levette Davidson quotes the *Denver Post* of May 21, 1950, which provides instructions on how to train a young burro for such a pack train.

> *Tie a short rope from the halter of the young burro to the tail of a gentle old burro. When the trainer starts the burrocade the young burro doesn't know what to do and stands until the old burro resents its tail being pulled and kicks the learner in the face. At the same time the trainer beats it on its rump with a club. It soon learns to put its head along the hip of the lead burro in order to avoid the double punishment.*

Francis Wood, wife of famous freighter Dave Wood, wrote of her first encounter with burros and it just happened to be a string of burros:

> *We passed the oddest-looking little woolly beasts of burden, nearly fifty of them in a line, each one tied to the one in front and heavily loaded with boxes and sacks of provisions for the mines. They were burros, and this was a burro pack train.*

Quite a few women mentioned seeing burros or burro trains in their diaries. Anne Ellis, author of *Life of an Ordinary Woman*, remembered the burro trains that she saw as a child, as they passed through the streets of Bonanza, which is now close to being a Colorado ghost town.

> *Going by our house are strings of burros with the panniers on either side full, on top of this a roll of bedding, then drills, picks and shovels on top of all. These are freight trains coming down with ore, or up with supplies, and the stage dashing through with passengers.*

Anne and her brothers and sisters took their burro with them when they went camping and fishing without adults along. The burro carried their supplies and stood guard over the children, who felt perfectly safe with it and their dog along.

Harriet F. Bacus, author of *Tomboy Bride*, had a more common meeting with the burro pack trains, but was just as excited about the experience:

> *About this time of year (summer), up to the (Tomboy) Basin came groups of sure-footed little burros, diminutive alongside the tall, big-boned mules. These "Rocky Mountain Canaries," as they were known, were not roped in strings. A skinner on horseback, assisted by his invaluable dog, drove them from the rear. Their little legs looked too small and delicate to support the loads which, though lighter and less unwieldy than those carried by mules, consisted of heavy boxes of powder, caps, fuses and such things.*

Harriet was noting that the burros did not come to Tomboy Basin in the winter. A burro will walk in the snow, if it is not too deep; but it will seldom walk on ice (which often covered the trail to Tomboy). Burros seem to realize that ice is slick and that they can easily fall and get hurt. If a burro does go out on ice, it proceeds very slowly and uses a funny shuffling maneuver, very similar to that used by humans who are afraid they might fall on ice.

Burros were sometimes trained to cover a regular path totally on their own. Several Colorado burros were reported to go by themselves to town to get supplies for their masters. The grocer would read the order they carried, then pack the provisions and send them back up to the mines on their own. A single burro that was with a man was seldom carrying freight for others, but was almost always carrying the supplies and baggage of the man it was with, who might be a prospector, a preacher, someone moving, or any other man who needed to have a load carried.

J. H. Little reported:

> It is a surprise to see under what heavy burdens these little creatures can plod along. I have seen a family moving from one town or camp to another with all of their household goods on the back of a single burro and the effects include a small coal-stove, a bedstead and bedding, two chairs, a grindstone and frame, and many pots, kettles, pans, and dishes. At the top of this prodigious pile was a baby, snuggly and securely fastened to the mattress of the bed.

Pack burros usually carried their load on a pack saddle, which consisted of two "X" frames (usually made of oak) attached to flat boards that ran between. A pack saddle could hold a canvas or leather bag full of ore on each side and another bag of ore or other container up top. The top position was a very good place for more fragile items. The two side bags (called "panniers") needed to be of about equal weight. If this could not be done, then the top load might make up the difference by sliding it one way or another. Seeing a burro being loaded like this was a little silly looking. One side of the pack saddle was loaded with ore or freight and the burro would look totally lopsided, like it would fall over at any time, until the other side was loaded with an equal weight and the burro could stand upright again.

Burro punchers figured out ways to get burros to carry almost anything. One man reported seeing a burro pack train from Del Norte that was making the week long, 110 mile trip to Silverton over Stony Pass — one of the steepest and roughest passes in all of Colorado. The pack train was carrying only one extremely large item, a full-sized billiard table that was strapped to the backs of twelve burros!

Leadville was still in its early boom times when this pack train of burros arrived about 1881.
Denver Public Library Western History Department (X-21776)

Burros carried other awkward loads, such as the early eight, ten, and twelve pound ore car track for the mines (the weight was per yard). When this was done, one end of the long piece of track was tied to the burro's pack saddle and the other end dragged in the dirt behind it. There might be one or two pieces of the lighter track on either side of the pack saddle. Burros also carried heavy, long timbers to the mine in this way, usually one piece strapped to each side of the pack saddle. Most timber was cut an inch or two longer than needed to allow for the lumber that would be worn off while being dragged along the trail. Sometimes, if a load was truly too heavy and too big for a single burro, a sling would be created between two burros, and the heavy or bulky item (like a large ore car) was put in the middle of the sling so that its weight could be split between the two animals.

When a burro was being packed, the freighters had to be especially careful, because many animals would expand their bellies by sucking in as much air as possible, and then let the air out after the cinch was supposedly tightened. The result was a loose cinch, and the whole load could fall to either side and have to be reloaded, invariably at a very inopportune time. To keep this from happening, packers would often kick or punch the burros in the belly right before tightening the cinch, which caused the animals to let the air out. It was a lot easier to pack a burro than a mule, because the burros were much lower to the ground.

Burros were generally not used for freighting in the winter in Colorado because of their very short legs and the deep snow; but it was a tradeoff if mules were utilized, as the burros were more sure-footed. The burro's sure-footedness and endurance was legendary. Burros were sometimes made use of by men who were traveling through deep snow in the winter and therefore could not carry any weight themselves. The men would have to break trail (pack down a trail in the snow) on foot or on horse-back, because of the burro's short legs, but the burro could carry blankets and other supplies that were absolutely necessary for winter travel. Often mules and burros had their shoes fitted with cleats in the winter to give them better traction on the slippery trails. It was often so cold at night that the burros were let inside whatever shelter the freighter was using. Prospectors' burros and the freighter's favorite burros were often invited inside the tent or cabin for the entire night. Freight burros would jockey for position around the camp fire in the winter to see which one would get the prime spots nearest the fire.

A few burros traveled in a very different way in the winter. It was reported by the Reverend George Darley that in the winter of 1879, a man simply had to get over Engineer Pass in deep snow, so he and his burro went from Mineral Point to Jack's Cabin (about five miles of very steep trail — all above timberline) with both on snowshoes made out of shoe leather. Darley said:

> It was slow work, but he succeeded in getting his jack across the range. This may sound 'fishy,' but it is the truth. Where a burro and a burro puncher cannot go, no other creature need try."

Many of the big but more remote mines tried to use burros year round. A. E. Reynolds bought the very rich Virginius Mine, which was over 1,000 feet higher in elevation than the little settlement of Sneffles, Colorado, itself at treeline. The Virginius claimed that it had "the highest post office in the world" at 12,500 feet — a service provided by burros until the snow got so deep that the only way to travel was by skis. Although rich, the Virginius was very hard to get to, even in the summer, and became almost impossible to access during the deep snows of winter (about four to six months of the year at that elevation). Reynolds used burros when he could, but eventually built the 7,800 foot long Revenue Tunnel to tap the Virginius ore at a much lower elevation that was close to that of Sneffles. Then he took millions in silver from the mine, much of it going down every day to Ouray (7,800-feet elevation) by mules and burros. A.E. Reynolds was one of the few owners or managers of a mine who recognized that the mules and burros that labored hauling ore from his mines actually worked better if given some rest; so he set his burros and mules on rotating "vacation time," during which they could simply graze and build up their strength.

Many men did not mine but just ran freighting companies. Dave Wood ran huge trains of pack animals between Ouray, Telluride, Montrose, Gunnison, and Lake City. He claimed that his was "the largest outfit in the West," and this may well have been true. John Ashenfelter started small but eventually built up a large freighting company that included about 300 burros as well as many mules, wagons and oxen. At its peak, his freight company alone carried 100,000 board feet of lumber and three million pounds of freight up the Camp Bird Road to the Camp Bird and Revenue Mines in one year. And, of course, an equal amount of ore came down. With all this activity going on, he kept a huge barn in Ouray and another large barn in Sneffles at the Revenue Tunnel.

Ashenfelter died in 1902, but John Donald carried on his work. Like Reynolds, Ashenfelter recognized the value of keeping his animals in good shape and even had a full-time veterinarian employed to treat hurt or sick animals, as well as a ranch where he kept injured or sick animals. Ashenfelter would fire a burro puncher on the spot who he felt was not taking care of his animals. This action was both a business and compassionate issue for him.

In some places, the burros were so numerous and important that they became a very integral part of the area's way of life. The town of Fairplay is proud of its burro heritage and has a full room in its museum dedicated to the homely burro. Over the years Fairplay had more freighting burros than any other town in Colorado, most of them in use before the Denver, South Park, and Pacific Railroad and the Denver and Rio Grande Railroad arrived in Leadville in 1880. Leadville was "just" over 13,185-foot Mosquito Pass from Fairplay. At times as many as 1,500 burros were on this trail at one time and

The burros being driven into Ouray carry ore from the Camp Bird or Revenue Mines. The cabin at right held powder and dynamite that citizens did not want in town.

Author's Collection

usually at least 1,000 of the little beasts of burden were at work every day during the early boom, packing from Fairplay to California Gulch, to the City of Leadville after 1878, and to other little mining towns and mines in the nearby mountains. There were so many burros in Fairplay that some blacksmiths set up an assembly line, hoisting the burros off the ground in slings when they needed new shoes and having two to four men working on them at a time.

Although not as large as the Fairplay-Leadville pack trains, teams of 300 to 500 burros were reported in Ouray, Silverton, Creede, Aspen, and Cripple Creek, as well as other large mining towns. Two of the big freight companies in the Silverton area were owned by Louis Wyman and Otto Mears. Wyman dedicated his office building to the burro and personally carved the relief of a burro over the main entrance to the building. Otto Mears is famous throughout the state of Colorado as a toll road and railroad man; but his businesses also included stores, hotels, and pack trains that employed both mules and burros. Freighter Ed Lavender ran about 100 animals out of Telluride every day to bring ore down from the famous Tomboy Mine. The Smuggler-Union Mine ran a similar sized pack train, although the neighboring Liberty Bell Mine used a tram from early in its operations. Rico, Ophir, Alma, Buckskin Joe, Georgetown — all of these towns had burro trains at work while waiting for wagon roads and railroads to arrive.

As John Cowan wrote at the beginning of the twentieth century:

> But it is not alone to the Mexican and the Indian, or to the prospector and the miner that the burro is a necessity and an ever-present help. The burro pack trains that may be seen in Hageman Pass, at Ouray, on Aspen Mountain, on the Gold Belt Trail, on the Funeral Range, the Calico and Telescope and Panamint Mountains, at Bullfrog, Manhattan, Fairview,

and a hundred other places tell the story of isolated camps far up in the mountains or away out on the inhospitable desert that depend wholly or in part upon the unlovely, but not entirely unlovable burro, for communication with the great world outside, even in these rushing days of railroad, telegraph and air-ship. Their toils in the treasure vaults of nature, or of lumber for the cabins of the miners, or for the dance halls, gambling joints, and saloons that belong insep-arably to the mining camps, or they may be ore bound for the smelter, or gold dust for the mint or the lifeless form of some poor devil who has "cashed it in," leav-ing money or dust enough to secure respect for his last wish that he be buried "back home." It is all the same to the patient animal that picks its way so gingerly along dizzy ledge, around and among tottering boulders, over scorching sands, or across sliding snows that need only an incautious footstep to transform them into an ava-lanche. A strange and anachronic mode of transporta-tion, this — in these swift days of steam and electricity — but a method that must survive along the backbone of the continent and in the arid lands of the Southwest for years or centuries to come.

Because of their endurance and ability to eat just about any-thing, burros were often used for very long trips. Their longest haul in Colorado was probably from the San Juan Mountains in southwestern Colorado to smelters in Denver or Pueblo, a two to three week trip of more than 200 miles each way, but necessary in the 1870s when there were no efficient smelters in the San Juan Mountains. The average freight rate from the San Juans to Pueblo dropped from $200 per ton to about $100 per ton in the late 1870s. This rate was somewhat constant until the Denver and Rio Grande Railroad made it into the San Luis Valley, when it dropped even further. Ore still had to be very

*One little burro knows exactly where to go and has already
outpaced the rest of the herd taking timbers to a mine.*
Photographer William Henry Jackson,
Colorado Historical Society (CHS.J978)

valuable to make a profit with such high freight costs, so only
the very richest ore could be sent out. Big mines hired scores of
men to do nothing but chip away low-grade or barren rock from
the rich ore. The low grade ore just piled up on the mine's dump
waiting for a cheaper form of transportation before it could be
transported.

Even with all the expense, in the 1870s there was a constant
stream of burros moving ore from Silverton or Lake City to Del
Norte and Ft. Garland, and then over LaVeta Pass to Pueblo or
Denver. Supplies and equipment were then carried back. One
unusual burden for a burro pack train was the load of bricks
that came into Silverton in 1874, which were to be used to build
George Greene's smelter. The freight cost was twenty-five cents
a pound, which made the total cost of one brick about a dollar
(about ten dollars each in today's money). The smelter was badly
needed, but unfortunately Greene could not get it to work properly at Silverton's extremely high altitude. By 1880 the Denver
and Rio Grande Railroad took over the burros' load in the San

Luis Valley; and by 1883 the D&RG was in Gunnison and Silverton, and the really long hauls by burro trains were no longer
needed. Later several good smelters were built in the San Juans,
with the best being in Durango. Many of the later-day mines
had trams that took the ore directly to the railroad, thereby
eliminating even the need for ore wagons pulled by mules.

It would be expected that the valuable burro would have
been treated well by the freighters, as it generally was by the
prospectors. However at the mines, on pack trails, and in other
forms of work such as in the tourist trade, burros were sometimes badly abused in many different ways. When a burro was
carrying supplies and equipment up to the mines, it was often
carrying dangerous substances such as dynamite, nitroglycerin,
oil, kerosene, acids, and blasting powder. If a burro's load blew
up, the little animal simply disintegrated. With leaking acids
and other caustic liquids, the animals could receive burns or
wounds that might leave them crippled and in pain for the rest
of their lives.

*Burros being loaded with ore sacks (located at left of photo) at a
mine above treeline near Ouray, Colorado, about 1885.*
Author's Collection

The ore the burros carried down from the mines was not only heavy but also unwieldy, and it usually had sharp edges. Since freight rates were based on the weight being carried, the burros were often overloaded, or at least, pushed to their limits. Even when using pack saddles with thick canvas or leather bags of ore tied to the "cross-buck," the ore still managed to poke and rub the animals constantly through the heavy bags. There was often, but not always, some type of padding under the pack saddle. It was also important to use the same pack saddles on an animal, so that the saddle could contour to fit the back of each individual burro. Unfortunately only a few burro punchers took this simple precaution and the packs would often rub the animal's back and cause sores. Many animals had sores that were very hard to heal unless the animal was given a few days off, which almost never happened.

Ellen Jack wrote of one extreme case:

> *I was sitting by my open window when a pack of jacks came by, going to the corral for the night, and as they passed the stench was fearful, and I noticed that some of them could barely walk. The jack punchers were yelling at their dogs to hurry them. I do not know what struck me, for I sprang out of my door and after the jacks. I stood outside of the board fence watching them take the pack saddles off of the poor animals, and such a stench and such a sight I cannot describe, for there was not one whose back was not raw as beefsteak. Two of the punchers got a piece of flat stick and scraped the maggots out of their wounds, and if the jacks moved, they kicked them or beat them unmercifully.*

Ellen reported the burro punchers to the newly hired Gunnison humane officers, filed charges, and the men were fined fifty dollars each and ordered to turn the jacks out to pasture until their wounds were healed.

As far as the miners were concerned, one of the most important cargos that a burro might carry in those days was whiskey, which was usually carried in barrels. Rev. John Dyer, one of the few Colorado pioneer ministers who had no burro (he rode a horse, skied or walked), wrote of one train he had encountered that was "attacked by prospectors" who were after a burro that was obviously carrying whiskey.

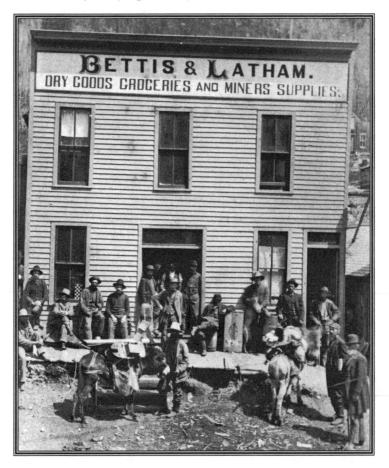

Golden was still a young town when this photograph of a large group of "hopefuls" was taken about 1860.
Denver Public Library Western History Department (X-9839)

They caught the burro, one holding it by its head, and
another by its tail, and the third trying to get the cork
out....Suffice it to say they all drank out of a tin cup,
and one of them poured out gold dust into the freight-
er's hand until he was satisfied.

As mentioned, burros did not like crossing water. One writer wrote "a burro's fear of water reminds one of a woman's fear of a mouse." One burro almost lost its life when a puncher forced it to go into an icy, fast-moving stream with an empty whiskey barrel on its back. Unfortunately, the barrel had no peg in its bunghole, the burro slipped, and the barrel started filling with water. With the extra weight and fast moving water, the burro could not get back on its feet; so the burro puncher jumped into the freezing water to get his burro back upright and the whiskey barrel draining instead of taking in water. Later, the man and his burro made it back to their cabin, but they were both nearly frozen and had icicles hanging from their bodies. The puncher let his burro into the cabin and per-mitted it to dry before the fire. He said it turned from one side to the other before the fire, just like a human would do. Then, when its fur was dry, it bolted out of the door of the cabin to join the other burros.

Summer or winter, if a burro stopped, or worse yet, laid down on the trail, the burro punchers quickly resorted to plead-ing, coaxing and swearing, which would almost always swiftly escalate into physical beatings accompanied by more and louder profanity from the burro puncher. As David Roberts pointed out, "This highly developed and perfected eloquence was con-sidered a prerequisite for the job (as a burro puncher), and it is doubtful success could be achieved by those deficient in this category."

Reverend George Darley heard the burro blamed so often for the profanity of the burro punchers that he felt compelled to write in defense of the burro:

*As a personal and particular friend of the faithful
beast that has done so much to help develop Colorado,
I regret that many believe that the burro has culti-
vated the (human) swearer as much as he has in the
state. Those who abuse the burro and swear at him
like a pirate, curse everything; not because they are
provoked, but because they are habitual swearers.
When men have excused themselves for cursing on
the grounds that a burro is a stubborn animal, I have
answered, 'Treat you as your burro is treated and you
will become as stubborn as he.'*

However this situation was usually the case of two very
obstinate and immovable creatures meeting, and the human of
the pair usually resorted to inhumane action and outright bru-
tality. Burros might be kicked, hit with large sticks or boards,
or harshly whipped. They were even hit with shovels and picks,
or guns were fired near their ears. All the while the profanity
continued. No amount of punishment seemed too harsh. Many
burro punchers actually thought the burro so hardy that it could
not feel pain or be killed; others said "they just dry up and blow
away."

Reverend George Darley reported that freighters seemed
to believe a burro had no feelings or emotions, and that they
expected mistreatment from man. Darley wrote, "Burros suffer
terribly, and if men are to be punished for cruelty to animals,
some men will discover that none of God's creatures can be tor-
tured, and the culprit go free."

Many accidents occurred along the trail. If a burro stepped
off the pack trail in the winter and sunk into the soft snow
along the side, it would usually not panic and would stay still
until it was rescued. Unfortunately, there were times when it
was impossible to get the burro back on the trail, and it had to
be shot where it lay stuck. A horse or a mule would be much
more likely to flounder in the snow, sinking ever deeper — often

making a rescue totally impossible and its death much more likely. Avalanches, freezing temperatures, and deep snow were all major winter dangers in the Colorado mountains. Over the years, literally thousands of burros and mules were swept off trails or down mountainsides by avalanches. In the spring it was not unusual to see dozens of rotting mule and burro carcasses below the steeper trails. Normally neither the burros nor their

Pack burros went out of Georgetown for years with loads of supplies for the mines in the nearby mountains. By this time (about 1880) the town was well-established.
Photographer Lachlan McLean, Denver Public Library
Western History Department (X-1363)

load could be rescued until spring, so the burros that were not shot on the spot died of hypothermia or starvation, if they had not been killed instantly by fast-moving, concrete-hard snow slides or a long fall on to the rocks below.

If any burro in a pack train went off at a steep point along the path and was tied to the other burros, it was possible that the whole string of burros might be pulled off the trail to their deaths. Some burro punchers used slip knots to tie the burros together, so the whole train could be released with a quick jerk of the rope that connected them. However this also allowed some of the animals to come loose when not in danger, so some burro punchers did not use slip knots. A burro train carrying tram or winze cable was also tied together with no way to separate the animals. Because of its weight, the cable was usually tied two loops to each side of a burro, and then continued the same way on down the line.

Freighters were often very creative in securing their loads to their animals, but they also liked to have some fun with the tenderfeet. One story goes that a burro was carrying a wheelbarrow packed upside down with the wheel in the air. A newcomer asked why the wheelbarrow was tied that way (as if there was another way to tie it on.) The freighter answered:

> *This here jassax has been acquired by old Walapai Huggins fer a house pet at the Bully Boy Mine, and bein' as the annimule is too dellycate to walk all the way over the rough trails, the old man drives him up hill an' at the summit jes' naturally turns him down on the other side. Yes sir, it DO come hard on old Walapai but it is mighty restin' fer the jassax.*

Burros carrying ore, sometimes did not make it to their destination with their payload, leading to many "lost ore" tales. For example, in the early 1890s, Al Stevens was a small-time freighter working with only seven burros in the area of Creede.

He did no mining himself but packed supplies and ore for some of the smaller mines. Over time Stevens became pretty good at recognizing rich ore (which he sometimes took instead of cash for his pay). Evidently he acted as if he was mentally disabled in order to disarm his customers. Although he had seven burros, he always rode one of them to the mines, carrying extra ore sacks with him, which he said were for emergencies if any of the mine's sacks tore. Stevens walked on the way down, but the burro he rode to the mine would always carry only two sacks filled with ore with the empty sacks on top of the load on the return trip. Stevens said he did this because of the extra weight that burro had to carry on the way up.

What Stevens was doing was taking a few pieces of high grade ore from the sacks his burros were carrying and putting the stolen ore in the "empty sacks," which he would later hide shortly before arriving back in Creede. At a later time he would take his stash of ore out of the area to be sold. When the Silver Panic of 1893 closed most of the silver mines around Creede, Stevens moved his operation to Bear Town, which was in the far southern San Juans where gold was being found. There he continued his stealing. A few pieces of gold ore from each sack could yield a lot more money than a few pieces of silver, but he had a problem — there were not nearly as many trees or gullies where he could hide his gold as at Creede. Still, by the end of the season he had seven totally full and very rich bags of ore, which he divided into twelve partially filled bags. He decided to take these bags to Pagosa Springs to be assayed and sold but did not follow any particular trail during his trip.

Somewhere between Wolf Creek Pass and Pagosa Springs he hid ten bags of ore in a hole he dug, and then he carefully covered them so that the ground did not look disturbed. He took the other two bags to Pagosa Springs where he sold them for $1,792 at $20 per ounce for gold. This amount would be over $100,000 at today's prices. But in the meantime it had started snowing in the high country, and it snowed so much that Stevens could not get back to the gold. When he finally returned the next spring he could not find his gold ore, which would be worth over a half million dollars today.

In 1933 a sheepherder found Steven's gold, but the bags had rotted and he was only able to fill his two pants pockets with ore. It assayed at an extremely high gold content, but the sheepherder died that winter without disclosing where he had made his rich discovery. Some have searched for the lost gold, but to date no one has found it.

Prospector and freight burros may have been the lucky asses. Burros were often used for work other than freighting at the mines. When pulling ore cars in the mines, the burros had a big advantage over a mule, because they were shorter. The mules were always bumping their heads on anything that extended below the top of the tunnel. Because regular mules were usually too tall to use in the mines, there was a special mule developed for mine work that was a cross between a small female wild mustang and a Spanish jack. The result was a much smaller animal than a regular mule (but it was a mule — a cross between a burro and a horse) called a "Spanish Mule."

Another reason that burros were used underground was that they were less likely to panic than a mule in a bad situation (such as a fire or a cave in). If something went wrong in the mine, a burro would usually stop to decide what action to take and then react appropriately. Burros always worked hard, but the Spanish mules could pull heavier loads and eventually were preferred for this work. The men who took charge of the mules and burros that pulled the ore cars in the mine were called "trammers." Just as with a burro puncher, these men had to understand their animals, and like the prospector they established a close relationship with their animals.

When burros or mules were worked below ground in mines, there was no major problem if the ore was accessed through a tunnel, but it could be a real challenge to get a mule or burro down a shaft and later to get it back out. Often they were

Tom May, a trammer, and his burro "January" in the Mendota Mine near Silver Plume about 1900. Note the carbide lights on January's back.
Denver Public Library Western History Department (X-17659)

treated as pets by the miners, who might feed them part of their lunch. Miners were also known to bring green grass or hay to their burro friends. But the poor animals lived most of their lives in total darkness and usually went blind (or were purposely blinded by driving nails or spikes into its eyes, because it was thought that burros would go mad if exposed to light again). Sometimes the burros that were no longer needed in the mine were killed and left there or cut into pieces and brought back to the surface. Many burros were also killed or injured while working in the mine by cave-ins, electrocution, deadly gases, fires, and other accidents.

Just as we cannot generalize about all burros, we cannot say that all men of this time mistreated their animals. Some men especially loved and understood the little beasts — especially ministers. There were even men who wrote the burros poetry — many more poems seem to have been written in Colorado about burros than horses and mules. Father J. J. Gibbons was enamored enough by the furry little creature to write a two page poem to the burro, part of which is at the beginning of this chapter.

The Mining World of October 6, 1906 carried a tribute to the burros' service to mining, pointing out that they were the perfect form of transportation to use while a new mine was being developed, thereby avoiding the large capital expenditures required to build a good road.

> *By the aid of that docile beast great wealth has been taken from remote places that knew not a wheeled vehicle of any sorts.... The first shipments of ore are frequently conveyed by burro train many miles along the mountain trails to a wagon or railroad and sometimes to the smelter itself.*

The idea of bringing burros back into the transportation system did not catch on well in the United States because of the infatuation with fast cars and trains, but the burro was still very popular for use in mining in South America. The same article lauded the strength, sure-footedness, and durability of the burro:

> *His weight does not usually exceed 600 pounds, but he will carry a load of 250 pounds over trails that seem utterly impassable ....If perchance he loses his footing and rolls into the canyon below, he scrambles up uninjured save for the humiliation of having to hurry.*

Then to top off all the praise, the article (remember this is a professional engineering journal) ended with another of the hundreds of printed poems dedicated to the burro, this one complete with prospector slang:

THE POOR, ABUSED OLD BURRO

There is one pore critter gits abused
an' cussed more'n all the rest;
Yet, size 'im up, of all the beasts he's jest about the best.
He don't stack up on beauty none — he's humbly's all git out;
But when thar's su'thin' to be done he'll always go the rout'.

His hide is gen'ly fuzzy, an' his ribs is plain in sight;
But then, he'll stay right by the game,
jest use him half way white;
A chance to browse, say one't a week,
as long's the fol'age lasts,
An' after that some ol' tin cans — that's all the critter asts.

His ears ain't ornamental — they take up too much room;
But he has done more'n his honest
share in many a mining boom.
He's staggered under loads that's weighed a blame'
sight more than him,
An' packed hull minin' outfits, from a geared hoist to a whim.

He'll climb the sides o' gulches that a squirrel couldn't scale —
Dive into canyons so blame steep that, let his footing fail.
Ye'd see the hull caboodle go clean down to kingdom come;
It 'twan't fer him the minin' world would sure be the bum!

Ye couldn't opened up yer claims without the critter's help;
Yet, notwithstandin' all he's done, ye treat him like a whelp.
Ye hate to hear him singin' in his dulcet tone o' voice,
An' cuss about it, jest as if the critter had a choice!

He took what nature give him, jest the same as me an' you;
An' mebbe he'll pan out the best, when all of us gits thru'.
But, anyway, he does his work, an' does it good an' thoro';
So what's the use o' kickin' on the pore, abused ol' burro!

But eventually the railroads served most of the big mines; and if there was no railroad, there would at least be a good wagon road. It was not too much later that trucks were hauling ore, eliminating animals altogether. The result was a large excess of burros. Wild burros roamed all over the hills of the nearby towns. During this time George Cowell, an old time prospector in Fairplay, recalled what happened next:

> *People would put their eggshells and coffee grounds and potato peelings out in the streets. About six o'clock at night the burros would come down out of the timber and eat up all this garbage, even the paper off the cans. Then they would go down to the saloons and drink from the watering trough. If you wanted a burro you never bought one. You picked one out and put your brand on him.*

A burro train carries food supplies on Aspen Mountain. A few other travelers also got their photo taken.

Photographer William Henry Jackson,
Colorado Historical Society (WHJ 950)

CHAPTER FIVE

ℒℴℑ

Any Port in a Storm
Women, Children, Clowns and the Burro

When burros were no longer needed in the mines, or by a prospector, or for whatever other work they were doing in the nineteenth century, many of them were simply let go. They were not even worth the money it would cost their owners to haul them to another area for a possible sale. The inquisitive, hardy animals would usually end up roaming the hills around a mining town, at times coming down to look for handouts from the townspeople. Many of the local women fed the little beasts leftover food, much like you would do with a pig or a goat.

These relationships usually worked out well for both parties, but some women had a love-hate relationship with the burros. They enjoyed the cute, little animals, and they relished the fun their children had with them; but if there was no fence around their yard, roaming burros would often get into their gardens and eat the vegetables and flowers. Burros also had a special affinity for eating greasy burlap bags and sacks that had held bacon or ham at one time. They could smell the bags from a mile off and would ransack around until they found these delicacies, leaving trash all over the yard or street. Burros were even known to eat laundry that had been hung out to dry; and one man swore that burros considered women's negligees as a real treat. Some burros were said to snap ropes, squeeze through fences, or break open wooden boxes to get to something they really wanted to eat.

A young woman shares a drink with a young burro. The title of the photo is "It Tastes Good to Me."
The Burro Book, Author's Collection

Dave Day, editor of Ouray's *Solid Muldoon* newspaper wrote of this tendency of burros to eat almost anything in a poem he wrote in the August 5, 1881 issue:

> *The burro is a pretty bird,*
> *And loves to dine on shirts;*
> *But for a mid-day luncheon*
> *Prefers to eat old skirts.*
> *Old petticoats and bloomers*
> *Appraise his appetite,*
> *While crinoline and corset*
> *Fill him with great delight*

Many women had picket fences around their homes and gardens just to protect against grazing burros. But sometimes this precaution was to no avail.

Alex Carey wrote of "Old Sid," who he said stood out from all the rest of the burros that roamed around Lake City in the 1930s and 1940s:

> *When the mines closed down more or less, they (burros) put in their time running around town g e t t i n g into all kinds of mischief. Getting into people's gardens, eating up the flowers and braying their heads off. They took a very special delight in getting under your bedroom window in the early morning hours and braying like the dickens....*
>
> *(Old Sid) traveled alone. With his years of experience, "Old Sid" was the smoothest gate opener of them all. A large white donkey with great long ears and large soulful eyes, always with a look of complete innocence on his face. Many the cussin' he received but his abilities were respected by all. If anyone from the outside had tried to steal him the whole town would have risen up in wrath.*

Everyday "Old Sid" made his rounds, going from gate to gate, the other donkeys often standing back watching, they respected his abilities too, and when he got a gate opened they would follow him in. When they had gained an entrance, it was just too bad for the garden if the people who lived there were not home to chase them out. They would eat their fill and what they didn't eat would be trampled and pushed back into the ground. "Old Sid" was good also at opening shed doors. One time, so the story goes, Joe Hunt had a nice bunch of chickens which were fed wheat that he kept in a shed with a good latch on it. None of the other donkeys, try as they would, could get into it. It was duck soup for Old Sid! He made it several times, eating up all the wheat, which donkeys love, and scattering the rest around just for the heck of it. Joe went up to town and bought more wheat every time and finally in desperation purchased a strong hasp and padlock. He put that on the door, locking it up tight, probably saying to himself, "Let's see you get into that, you old so and so." That evening as Joe and his wife were eating their evening meal, he happened to look out the window ... "Look at that," Joe shouted to his wife, pointing at Old Sid. "Look at that damned donkey trying to find where I hid the key!"

Yet, even with all the problems that burros could cause, most women loved the little animal, and women often got together and took trips into the mountains for picnics and other activities on the local burros. Most women preferred to ride the burro rather than a horse, as they usually rode side saddle on their more "laid back" burro and felt safer than if riding a tall, high-strung horse. Burros rarely bucked and were not as "explosive" as a horse if they did. They also were not as inclined to bolt if spooked, and if they were to bolt they would usually not go far.

Ten Ouray women are getting ready for a side-saddle ride into the mountains on burros about 1900.

Author's Collection

The women were closer to the ground on a burro and much less likely to get hurt. Some of the more avant-garde women would ride astride the burro, even though they would not have thought of riding in such a manner on a horse. Some women had little two wheel carts that were pulled by burros to take them around town without the dangers of a runaway horse.

There are many classic old photographs of a dozen or so women in black dresses riding side-saddle on their burros. Why the fashion was to wear black dresses on these dusty outings remains a mystery to these authors, but the women always seem to have them on and many women also wore cone-shaped hats. Often, when on an outing, a woman's very young children rode in wooden boxes strapped to a burro's back — a kind of car seat of the nineteenth century. This action showed the trust these women had in the gentleness and dependability of their burro. As one early author put it in the stiff Victorian writing of the time, "Women and burros seem to complement each other in work and have shared companionship."

On the other hand, many American men did not see the burro as a riding animal for men. J. H. Lewis wrote:

> Nothing but actual necessity ever induced the traveler, or anyone else, to ride the burro from one place to another. The little animal's usefulness in this direction is greatly impaired by his diminutive size and his unalterable determination never to go faster than a slow walk.... His gait is so tedious that the man who mounts him is soon glad to dismount and go further and faster on his own legs. A tall man makes himself especially an object of ridicule when astride a burro.

One of the most famous of all "burro punchers" was a woman, Olga Schaff, who was raised on a ranch near Durango by her immigrant German parents who had moved there in 1898. Olga and her brother were breaking wild horses by the time she was fourteen. Then Olga drove the livery teams, taking tourists into the mountains for the day, like today's jeep tours. In 1909 she was talked into taking a mule train to a mine after the wagon road washed out. Olga continued as a burro puncher and did her job well. She treated her burros with respect and admiration. She almost froze to death that same year when she fought through deep snows to bring food supplies to three stranded miners but then found she could not get back out. There was plenty to eat, but nothing to keep the group warm. The miners and Olga did eventually get out alive and well.

In 1911 Olga was snowed in with sixteen miners at the Neglected Mine. She fed oatmeal to her burros for five days, as it was the only food available. Olga and eleven of the miners eventually made it to the Transfer Mine five miles away, but it is said that the miners only made it because of Olga's prodding. The only food at the Transfer was crackers and eggs, which Olga and five men took to the miners who had stayed at the Neglected Mine. At the age of twenty-six Olga married William C. Little,

Olga Little packs her burros for a trip into the mountains about 1925.

Center for Southwest Studies, Ft. Lewis College

who had met her in 1913 when he was a mine owner who needed a packer. After he and Olga married, he became a burro puncher as well, and they increased their pack team to forty animals. Bill retired in the 1940s to cut, polish, and sell minerals.

Olga was probably the only woman burro puncher in all of Colorado, and she often worked by herself and had to keep her animals tied together. She used slipknots for the rope connecting the animals and the loads being carried, so that the animals and the loads were easy to release if any animals were in trouble. She was well respected by her contemporaries and was considered one of the best, if not the best, burro puncher in southwest Colorado at the time. She made five dollars a ton for hauling ore to the smelter at Durango. The ore was carried seventy pounds to a sack and three sacks to a burro, so with her thirty to forty burros she made about fifteen to twenty dollars for a one to two day trip. This was very good pay for a woman in those days. Olga was famous enough that she was written about in the December, 1949, *American Magazine*, and she also appeared on the television show *This is Your Life*.

For more than thirty years Olga ran her burros all over the La Plata Mountains in the southern part of Colorado, usually around Durango and Cortez; and occasionally she took her pack train all the way to Pueblo. By the time Olga retired in the early 1950s, the burro had almost vanished from Colorado. Federal agricultural statistics showed only 600 domesticated burros in the entire state of Colorado at the time; but the census takers probably did not include wild burros in the count, although there were not many of them either.

Olga was different from most freighters — she truly loved her burros. On one of her trips, the burro at the end of the line slipped, broke loose from the rest of the pack train, and went over the side of a steep precipice with two large boards tied to its back acting like runners on a sled. The burro went on an unwanted sled ride all the way to the very bottom of the canyon. Unfortunately, there was no way to get the burro out in the winter. Most male burro punchers would have shot the animal or left the burro there to die of starvation or the cold, but Olga brought her burro hay every week and the animal ate snow for water. This allowed the animal to live until spring when Olga got him out alive. In the latter part of her career, Olga switched to using mules and wagons, but she kept and continued to care for the burros that had been in her burro trains for the rest of their lives.

Another event that showed Olga's love of her animals was the time her lead horse stepped off the edge of the trail and skidded and rolled 1,000 feet down a steep slope. Olga went down and covered the animal with a blanket but knew she would not be able to get the animal out by herself, so she gave him hay and made him comfortable. She then went back to the trail and dug a small snow cave in which she spent the night next to her burros. The next day she went for help and dug her horse out.

Another woman who lived the man's life of a prospector with her burros was Caroline Moorehouse. A widow with two children, she somehow still managed to prospect for years for gold and silver in the Buena Vista area. She said that she was told where to dig for the precious minerals by spirits. Whatever the reason for her success, she recorded fifteen valuable mining claims in her name over the years and became both a well-respected woman and a well-off prospector. She retired in leisure and died in 1902.

Mollie Kathleen Gortner was yet another woman who struck it rich. Mollie was not really a prospector but was visiting her son at the new mining camp of Cripple Creek in 1891, when she decided to take a burro and see if she could locate an elk herd he had mentioned. While sitting down to rest, she noticed a rock ledge that looked very similar to the rich Cripple Creek gold ore that her son had shown her. Her son confirmed the rich discovery, but she was told by local prospectors that she could not file a claim because she was a woman. She did so anyway, thereby officially locating one of the most famous mines in the Cripple Creek Mining District — the Mollie Kathleen Mine.

Perhaps one of the strangest women who was involved with burros was Ellen Jack, also known as "Captain Jack." Ellen was born in England, married an American sea captain, and immigrated to Colorado after her husband's early death. She eventually had prospectors explain how to find rich ore and ended up part owner of the Black Queen, a rich mine located between Crested Butte and Aspen, where she helped run the burro pack train carrying her ore out and supplies in. She even credited herself with saving the men at the mine when she was supposedly the only person at the mine who had the nerve to take a burro train for badly needed supplies in the middle of a deadly snowstorm.

Ellen noted that the jacks coming from Aspen to Crested Butte were carrying 300 pounds of ore and that they were used in the winter. She later wrote:

The jacks had bells on their necks, and the tinkling of the bells and the barking of the dogs and the cursing of the jack punchers behind a train of jacks keeps a camp pretty lively.

After leaving the Gunnison-Aspen area, "Captain Jack" opened a "mine" (actually more of a cut into the local rock) tour and gave tourists rides on her burros near Colorado Springs. She loved to present herself as an authentic pioneer Westerner

Captain Jack was a very unusual woman who used a gun, kept a string of burros, and became a tourist attraction in later life outside Colorado Springs.

From Fate of a Fairy, Author's Collection

(which she was, although a very eccentric one) and get her photo taken with the tourists and her burros. Many a burro tour into the mountains around Colorado Springs or Manitou Springs ended up at Captain Jack's place in the mountains. Even the Broadmoor Hotel provided horseback and burro rides to Captain Jack's place. The positive side of Captain Jack's eccentric actions was that she represented an important era in Colorado history and made the tourists aware of the fuzzy, little burro.

As indicated previously, burros were used in many different endeavors other than mining — to pull carts, wagons, even small railroad "push carts." Sometimes the burro would pull the railroad cart uphill and then get a ride on the way down. "Vanderbilt" was a burro who worked for the Denver, Leadville and Gunnison Railroad. Vanderbilt was on duty at a section house between Fairplay and Alma. The burro would pull the railroad workers in the railroad's push cart up the grade, so the men did not have to do any pumping. Then, after the men's work was finished, they would sometimes let Vanderbilt ride on the cart on the way down when no pumping was necessary. The men also hooked some "snow flanges" to Vanderbilt's legs, so that the jack could help clear snow as it walked up the railroad tracks. Burros, like Vanderbilt, worked well when given routine tasks to their liking. Sometimes they might be loaded or hooked up and they would then start off on their own to do their task or go to their destination.

Burros were used to pull small wagons and carts which men and boys used for selling different commodities such as ice or vegetables. They were especially a favorite of those who brought drinking water to the mining camps before water systems were built, although large dogs were sometimes used. There are tales of both the dogs and burros being rewarded at the end of a day's work with a good shot of whiskey. Burros helped to bring in the lumber and hardware to build the towns to which they later brought food and other supplies. Burros even helped to build the wagon roads and the railroad grades that allowed mules, wagons, and railroads to eventually replace them at their jobs.

Just like the early Spanish padres, almost all of Colorado's early circuit riding preachers seemed to use the modest little burro for transportation at one time or another, and they are mentioned often and fondly in their owner's diaries and memoirs. Reverend George Darley wrote:

> *Often have I walked behind a burro when going to preach the Gospel in the "Region Beyond".... (Burros) were patient, sure-footed, and valuable, although greatly abused.... Some who are now counted among the 'leading lights' in Colorado were glad to have a*

Arthur Chapman, author of "Out Where the West Begins," poses on an Argentine Central Railroad cart with a burro foal about 1910.
Photographer Louis McClure, Denver Public Library
Western History Department (MCC-694)

burro carry their grub and blankets. ... This was considered a safe way to travel considering the roughness of the terrain.

However, burros could cause their minister owners all kinds of distress. The *Denver Times* of June 1, 1871, reported that in the Clear Creek Mining District a preacher had just reached the dramatic climax of his Sunday sermon, quoting the words from the bible, "Hark, I hear an angel sing," when a nearby burro let loose with its wondrous song. The congregation broke into hysterical laughter that reportedly seemed to last forever.

Reverend Darley reported that one Sunday evening when he was preaching, his son's burro, Maude, broke into song:

First a solo — low, clear, penetrating, not altogether unmusical; then a kind of duet, the outgoing breath making one kind of noise, the incoming another. This was followed by a quartet composed of the most hideous noises that it was possible for any of her species to make. By that time I (Darley) had stopped, but Maude, true to her nature, continued. The congregation could not contain themselves, for the burros of the neighborhood began answering, and I really think from the way that Maude then let out her voice that she thought it was an encore.

Burros were also used on Colorado ranches, where they might be tied by a short rope to an unbroken horse to help make the horse more manageable or to help train young stallions. They were only tied together for about thirty minutes, and the horse was usually combed and curried during this time. The poor burro did not get any attention. The idea was to get the horse to trust the men who came to care for it. Sometimes burros were even tied to bulls to try to get the bulls to calm down.

But there was another much darker side to the way burros were treated on some of the cattle ranches, where the horse was much better thought of and much better treated than the burro. Some cowboys actually hated burros. William Raines and Will Barnes in their books, *Cattle*, show just how inhumane man's treatment of the burro could be (and evidently still is in some areas of this country). They tell the story of a cattleman who had two of his cows killed by wolves. He instructed two of his cowboys to take a mother burro and her one-month-old foal to where the dead cattle had been found. The men knew that burro meat was the wolf's favorite treat. They killed the mother burro by hitting her in the head with an ax, then cut her body into pieces and put strychnine poison on all the meat. They also set steel traps all around the area using parts of the dead mother burro for bait. Then they rode away.

The baby burro followed the men for a short distance, braying at the top of his small voice, then suddenly turned and raced back to the spot where his mother lay. Throughout the long night the orphaned burro raised his voice on the clear night air, crying for attention from his dead mother. That was exactly what the rancher had hoped for. The crying of the burrito would attract the wolves to the poisoned flesh and the steel traps. Somehow the baby burro survived the night and the next day was taken back to the ranch house, where it was raised on a bottle.

Some people used burros for target practice to get ready for deer and elk season. (Lake City citizens report that the last wild burros in their area were killed in this way.) Often feral burros were killed *en mass* and their meat was sold for dog food. A few people were even reported to have served burro meat to unsuspecting diners as a joke.

One early practice involved burros being used in a manner similar to the way today's teenagers might try to find out how many people can be stuffed into a Volkswagen. The object was to see how many children or adults could ride on a burro at one time. The worst photographic example seen by these authors shows five people on the back of a donkey that is pulling a small wagon with thirteen more children as its cargo. The most a burro by itself could possibly hold was about eight, and one boy in that photo had to hang from the burro's neck.

Despite the abuses, the burro forgave quickly and did not seem to hold a grudge. Many other animals would have attacked the people abusing them or refused to be ridden again. It was

Someone managed to get six children on this burro, but with a little more effort they might have put one more at the front and perhaps another at the rear.

The Burro Book, Author's Collection

almost like the burros expected this kind of treatment, a fact which too many of their owners believed, or perhaps burros are just very forgiving and a good example of unconditional love.

Burros and children of all ages actually seem to be made for each other. One writer of the time wrote that burros and children go together like strawberries and cream. Burros love children and children love burros. Photographs showing small babies and burros together were very common in the nineteenth century. Even very young children were shown asleep with sleeping burros. One Colorado author wrote very picturesquely in *The Burro Book*, "The mountaineer's baby shared his meal with baby burros, and they slept together under the pines." Despite sometimes mistreating them, almost all children treasured their burro friends in the nineteenth century. Many of the memoirs of early Colorado pioneers who lived in the mining areas contain at least a paragraph or two about their childhood burro. For example, William Wardell wrote in his *Memories of Aspen, Colorado*:

> We children always had a burro to ride to school if we could catch one. It was not thought unusual to catch a burro and ride him for his feed. When a burro puncher was ready for his animals, he simply rode around town and gathered up those which had his brand. No one ever thought of stealing a burro, and the puncher was glad to have someone feed the animal, for it saved him the expense.

The children would ride their burros to school, and the animals would wait patiently for their riders during the entire school day and then take them home. If it was especially cold most children would bring a burlap sack or heavy canvas to cover their burro, but many of the little animals waited without complaint, without covers, without food or drink, and shivering in the cold and snow until the children were released from school.

This little boy is dressed up to play prospector, complete with a young burro loaded with the prospector's tools.
The Burro Book, Author's Collection

A large number of early Colorado photos exist of burros and children working or playing together. The very fact that there are so many of these photographs shows the strong connection. Burros were often shown pulling children in authentic but very small wagons — the forerunner of today's "little red wagon." Children might have burro rides available for their invited guests at a birthday party, or maybe the whole group would go up into the mountains, each child on a burro. Many families would have a small corral behind the house for keeping their children's burro. There seldom was a barn, usually only a little shed or lean-to, if anything, to keep the animal out of the weather. Burros helped children fetch water from nearby springs or creeks. They were also used to deliver groceries around town or to help with any of a boy's chores or duties, like taking garbage to the town dump.

Burros helped to pull children on snowshoes (today's skis) up the nearby hills, so they could ski back down, thereby taking the hard part out of the sport. The same little animal that slaved in the mines pulling ore cars also pulled laughing children up

This was the water system for Nevadaville, Colorado in Gilpin County in 1914. The boy is selling water for twenty cents for two thirteen-gallon barrels.

Denver Public Library Western History Collection (X-1248)

steep slopes to help them sled in the winter. They became so popular with children that burro children's books began being published as early as the 1890s, and burros showed up as favorite children's props in photographer studios. The previously mentioned *Burro Book* reads:

> *The children all love him. The little Indian plays round his heels without concern, the tiny Mexican wreathes his neck with yucca bloom, while the eastern child visitor proudly mounts upon his back and belabors him into a gentle walk, which is afterwards described as a "burro ride.*

Roger Henn, in his book *Lies, Legends and Lore of the San Juans*, describes the burros that were all over his hometown of Ouray, Colorado, when he was a boy in the 1930s:

*Burros thoroughly occupied Ouray. They were pick-
eted in every vacant lot; the corrals at the stables were
filled with them; and housewives were hard put to keep
loose burros from eating the flowers and vegetables in
the garden... Nearly every boy in Ouray had his own
burro since they were cheap — even free — and their
care cost little....*

*In some ways those burros raised us. For example,
if we mistreated (my burro) Queenie when we tried to
get her to go faster than she thought she should, she
would simply flop down on the ground, capturing at
least one of our legs under her... When Queenie was
sure we had been punished enough, she would rise
with dignity, permitting us to get in the saddle, and
would go placidly on her way, which we would hope
would be the same way that we wanted to go.....*

Roger also wrote that most of the burros that grazed around
Ouray wore bells, so that they could be heard when it came time

*Early Colorado children did not just use burros for riding. These
kids used their burro as the fulcrum for a see-saw.*
Ouray County Historical Society

to catch them. But Henn further reported that when the burros were being sought by the men who wanted to put them back to work, most of the burros would hide and stand absolutely still so that the bells would not ring.

But most of all, the ownership of a burro was a symbol to children that they were growing up, and it was also a means of transportation like today's teenagers' first car. The burro not only gave children a new found freedom (although somewhat limited), but also gave them an opportunity to make money. Many of the children used the burro in their paper routes for the local paper and the *Denver Post*. This allowed them to carry more papers and cover their route faster, while having some fun at the same time. The *Denver Post* in the late 1890s paid $1.00 to $1.25 per week for paper delivery — a good wage for a child who could get candy for a penny. The *Post* reported that almost every mountain town in Colorado had at least one newsboy using a burro to deliver the paper all the way up until the late 1940s.

Seventeen Denver Post *newspaper boys get their photo taken. Five of them evidently used burros for delivering the paper.*
Photographer Erickson, Author's Collection

In several ways the burro was the Rodney Dangerfield of the western animal world. Some writers, like J. H. Lewis, felt the burro to be "stupid, sleepy, and slow moving," but even Lewis admitted that the burro "has been an important factor in the development and growth of many mountain districts in the West." Not only did it "not get any respect," but it was also often used for comic relief, which often caused the burro terrible suffering, pain, and hardships only to be laughed at by the people that saw its predicament. The burro was the butt of way too many jokes, as well as the victim of way too much abuse in the name of humor.

Burros were made fun of in many ways, and they usually withstood their indignities without complaint. Dressing them up in costumes was often done — dresses, pants, and women's hats seemed to be the most popular attire; but they also wore derby hats and had cigars, flowers, and cigarettes put in their mouths for a photo to be taken (it was a real race to see if the photograph could be taken before the burro ate anything that might be placed in its mouth).

Prospectors got their photos taken with the burros when they were obviously drunk (the prospector, not the burro); or the burro was "bellyed up" to the bar for a photograph with all the "boys." It was also popular to get some greenhorn to try to ride a burro that no one could ride (this kind of burro was hard to find because almost all burros were easy to ride). Later, women got their photographs taken while talking on the telephone — one phone hooked to the burro's head and the other to its tail.

Rodeos and Wild West Shows often used the burro for comic entertainment. The burro would come out of the chutes with its rider dressed to the hilt as a cowboy and trying to lasso a steer or bulldog a calf. Maybe a burro and its rider might even be slipped into a bull riding contest. Many rodeo clowns rode a burro, while doing the very important and dangerous work of making sure that a bull did not hurt its rider, yet many

The boys at the White House Saloon in Cripple Creek (including the Sheriff) have invited their pet – a burro – to belly up to the bar.
Photographer William J. Gillen, Denver Public Library
Western History Department (X-661)

burros were hurt during this experience. Burros were hitched to chariots, goat carts, and full-sized wagons. Children loved to ride in these vehicles during parades. Tourist families almost always had a burro ride, as it was usually on the top of their lists of things they wanted to do while on vacation in Colorado (kind of like driving a 4-wheeler or riding a mountain bike might be today).

Buffalo Bill's Wild West Show used burros. As tall a cowboy as could be found was usually riding the smallest burro in the show, either in the arena or in the parades to advertise the show. Sometimes Buffalo Bill himself was on the burro. This always got a good laugh. Since his show went overseas, Buffalo Bill got to show off the little Mexican burro to the European crowd. Everyone loved them, although genetically the burros were just the same as the European donkeys. Burros were also used to help market movies like Charlie Chaplin's "The Gold Rush."

Burros were often ridden by children in Fourth of July parades. Men riding burros usually dressed up as clowns and rode the burro backwards, or perhaps the clown stood on two burros at the same time. Another favorite gimmick was to have a carrot tied by a string to a long stick which was held in front of the burro to encourage it onward, perhaps with someone else at the other end of the burro, holding its tail to try to keep it back.

Ouray resident Roger Henn wrote:

> *For boys who were burro owners, the Fourth of July celebration was most important. Every boy entered his burro into the burro races…. One never knew what a burro would do amid the shouting, noisy crowd; the results were often hilarious….*

Circus clowns at the Sunflower Carnival in Colorado Springs in 1898 seemed to prefer the burro 5 to 1 over the horse.
Photographer H. S. Poley, Denver Public Library
Western History Department (P-2234)

This photo at the top of Pikes Peak (14,147 feet) shows the old way (burro) of getting to the top and the new way (cog railroad) about 1885.

The Burro Book, Author's Collection

Although both were often mistreated by humans, dogs and burros seemed to get along well. Burros also were good company for horses and mules. Many of the older Colorado photographs that show a woman or children with a burro also include a dog in the photo. Horses and mules were much more afraid of dogs than burros were.

In 1873 Anna Dickerson rode burros up most of Colorado's non-technical fourteen thousand foot mountains — Pike's Peak, Grays, Lincoln, and Elbert to name a few. Many mountaineers, including the early U. S. Geological Survey crews, rode burros as far as they could (usually to about 11,000 to 12,000 feet), before climbing the rest of the mountain on foot. Early climbers noted holes dug by prospectors near the tops of the mountains. The prospectors probably had their burros with them.

By the early 1900s many burros were used in the tourist trade, and some photographers, who didn't want the trouble of live burros, even killed and stuffed them to help present an "authentic Old West atmosphere" on their sets. Other burros were used as "kiddy rides," an action that riled the few long-time prospectors who were still left in Colorado. One Fairplay prospector told the *Denver Post* (May 25, 1949):

> *Us mountain fellers have an old sayin' that a burro never dies. His life is nuthin' but fleas, skinned hide, ragged ears, rocky trails, slide diggin's, flapjacks and prunes, columbines and mountain grass, cussin' and snow, wind, rain and sun.*
>
> *Give them a full bag of oats evey day, good pasture, and tender, lovin' care from a passel o' kids and they won't live a week. I ain't condemning no string of mine to a ridin' circle.*

The burro was so well-known that it was instrumental in bringing early day tourists to Colorado. Not only could burros transport their riders into the high mountains, but they could

This group of tourists in Eldora Springs in 1910 seem to be having a great time, but their burros do not seem too impressed.
Photographer Robert Rockwell, Denver Public Library
Western History Department (X-8141)

do it in a safer manner than on a high strung horse. Yet many tourist burros were also badly abused by their owners, and many were mistreated on riding trips by tourists who did not understand the burro. The burro's passengers were certainly not going to give it credit for knowing more than they did about the rugged terrain, and the burro would sometimes be unmercifully beaten in an attempt to get it to do something that the burro knew it had no business doing. Children would pull its ears or tail and punch fingers in its eyes.

But apparently the tourists, old and young, loved their burro rides. Thousands of vintage photographs still exist of Colorado tourists proudly seated on their small, rented burros, especially from the area encompassed by the towns of Colorado Springs, Manitou Springs, and the Garden of the Gods. A ride to the top of Pikes Peak from Manitou Springs was probably the favorite tour that a tourist could take on a burro. In 1908 it cost $2.50 to rent a burro and ride to the top of "America's Mountain" from Manitou Springs. Many of the greenhorn travelers were so sore by the time they got to the top of the mountain that they took the $5.00 cog railroad back down.

The Denver and Rio Grande Railroad's "Circle Route Tour" was one of the most popular tours in Colorado from the 1880s to the 1920s. The tour allowed vistors to take a loop by train around Colorado's mountains that could be done anytime within a thirty day period. Although most of the tour was by narrow gauge train, there was a short section between Ouray and Silverton that was by stagecoach — advertised as "a real relic from the past." The railroad's brochure mentioned that 'likely enough a prospecting outfit with a pack train of burros is encountered," and "not only a burro might be spotted on this part of the route, but a prospector might be with him." The Denver and Rio Grande Circle Route Tour ran until the Great Depression, which along with the automobile, sealed its fate.

One never-to-be-repeated case of combining two tourist tours happened in 1895, when a group of women visitors that had ridden up from Manitou Springs on burros was allowed to ride the animals into the Cave of the Winds. Unfortunately, one of the women was thrown from her burro when the animal spotted stalactites in Canopy Hall, which it quite innocently assumed to be carrots. Everyone, except the woman who was thrown, had a good laugh, but the tour operator quickly got the burros out of the cave.

Yet another poet felt moved to write a poem about the burro's plight with the tourist:

A Burro's Rhapsody

A lone burro stood near a dark pine wood,
Where the trail was icy and steep,
And sang loud his praise of these stormy days,
When the mountains are wrapped in sleep....

Burros were used in many different ways, including
transportation for this bride about 1895.
Denver Public Library Western History Department (X-29437)

His tough back so sore and his lank sides bore
Deep marks of the whip and spur
Which riders in rage had left as a page
Of annals of pain as it were;
His sad notes resound on the night air 'round,
And great billows of melodies roam;
That far distant plain sends back the refrain,
When the tourists have all gone home.

Author Unknown, 1894

With such an excess of animals roaming free around the mountains of Colorado, burros ended up being used for all types of work that they might not have been used for if they had to be purchased. For example, burros were sometimes used for logging — hauling the necessary tools to the site, pulling the cut trees to sawmills, and taking the finished product from the mills to the mining camps and mines.

One unusual use for burros took place at the finely built and kept Silverton horse tracks, where they were regularly raced for money. Since the burro does not like to go fast and tends to slow down when encouraged to go faster, this type of event does not sound like it would be much to the burro's liking; although it must have had its hilarious moments for the spectators. The track also raced horses, mules, ponies, trotters, and even the town's firemen, who held their fire cart races there.

Another job that burros were not usually used for was carrying the U. S. mail. The mule and the horse were much faster and the loads generally were not heavy. But there were times when the loads were heavy or the trails so steep that burros were called into duty. The town of Silverton relied almost exclusively on burros to deliver the mail in the 1870s, as it was a 110 mile trip from Del Norte over very steep trails. Eventually, the railroad took over this task, but burros were still used to get the mail to the little post offices further up in the mountains, and they were often brought back into use when the train could not get the mail to Silverton because of avalanches or deep snow.

After World War II, the burro population began to decline rapidly in Colorado. It seemed (perhaps rightly so) that, unlike the mule, there was no good use for them in the state. Instead of letting them live out their lives in the mountains or go to a good home, many burros were killed. What was it that brought this type of reprisal on the lowly burro that had done no one harm? Why did we want to get rid of an animal that had done so much for Colorado? Why did we not return the faith, trust, and love

Two burros listen intently to music from an early phonograph at the Granby depot about 1910. Burros love music.
Denver Public Library Western History Department

that the burro had shown us? The answer is probably found in its traits of gentleness, humility, vulnerability, and innocence. Unfortunately it seems to be the nature of some humans to pick on those animals (and humans) that they perceive to be mild and meek. It was Mahatma Gandhi who said, "The greatness of a nation and its moral progress can be judged by the way it treats its animals."

CHAPTER SIX

ΩΩ

Out of Work
But Not Totally Forgotten

As reports of new discoveries of precious minerals slowed down in Colorado, and as wagons moved across newly built roads and the little narrow gauge trains puffed high into the mountains to take over the transportation business of the working mines, burros were still an accepted form of transportation. The ore had to be brought down from the more remote mines to the railroads and supplies needed to be taken back up on the return trip; but the distances covered were much shorter, and the number of burros needed for these tasks was greatly reduced. Then, as the trails got better, more and more burros were replaced by mules because they could carry much bigger loads. As geologist Mel Griffith wrote:

> *It was inevitable that the mule would ease out the*
> *burro for packing. If the burro was the logical choice*

for a low-budget prospector trip, the mule had unique advantages when packing became a high-volume business.

Then, with the advent of the automobile and the truck in the 1910s and 1920s, mules and burros served no useful mining function in Colorado, except for use in extremely remote areas of the state, where a few old prospectors still acted on their life-long dream to "strike it rich." The mules that were laid off still had jobs, as they could be used on farms and ranches, but most of the burros were abandoned, left to run wild and make it on their own. Many of them starved to death, were shot as nuisances, or were killed for pet food; but a few burros did survive and in some areas (usually very remote or arid) even multiplied their population.

In Fairplay, Colorado, the "Burro Capital of the World," large numbers of burros started to roam loose over the nearby hills by 1900. Many of the locals became angry at the braying that went on all day and all night. The burros were considered a major nuisance, and some citizens tried to get the town to do something about the situation. This time, however, a few people came to the burro's defense. The editor of the *Fairplay Flume* noted in his January, 1900 issue that many of the local burros were starving that winter and pointed out that, "There is no dumb animal in the Universe that meets with as much abuse and neglect as the burro of Colorado." Most of the people in Fairplay changed their attitude. Some of the Cripple Creek citizens, although still facing the same problems with the burros, responded to the starving animals by protecting them — an action that has been kept up to this day.

On the other hand, in August, 1901, Manitou Springs passed an ordinance that burros and any other animal that made "raucous noise" could not be kept within the city limits, and those burros that were found wandering loose in town were to be shot on the spot. Some of the more remote Colorado towns, like

Ouray and Silverton in the San Juans, were still using burros as pack animals at the time, so some unwanted burros were sold to freighters in those areas. However, there was no doubt that Colorado was trying to reduce a major surplus of burros, so the number of domesticated burros began to quickly decline.

Feral burros did not fare any better. Henry Rogers wrote in *The History of the Pike National Forest* that a local resident told him that there were 2,000 wild burros roaming between Fairplay and Cañon City in the early 1900s. Rogers claimed to have shot 100 burros in a single day at a remote spring. He also wrote that the cowboys would keep the burros away from water until the animals were extremely thirsty and then hide and shoot them for sport as they came in for a drink. Rogers wrote that there were a lot of dead burro bones around the South Park water holes — a reminder of the many burros that had been shot. In fact, there were so many bones that they were eventually collected and sold to companies for bone ash (used in making cupolas for assaying).

Colorado's mining boom days were basically gone by 1910, and with that period went the thrill of the prospector and their burro partners that had rushed from one new gold or silver discovery to another. It was only on occasion that there would be some short term need for burros. A resurgence of mining in Colorado occurred around World War I, and with it there was renewed interest in the use of burros. Surprisingly, the engineer was one of those at the forefront of promoting the proven little burro instead of new-fangled machinery, like the truck. An article in *Mining News* in 1914 quoted an address of William Burr to the Northern California and Southern Oregon Mining Congress in part:

> *The burro fills a place in the mining and metallurgical world that no machine can entirely fill.... He can ascend the loftiest peaks with his load and climb to places with comparative ease that a man can only*

*reach with difficulty.... He is almost as easy to raise
as a chicken, and is broken under the pack in one day.
His rate of travel loaded, for inferior animals is seven
miles, and for animals in good shape fourteen miles;
the average is eleven miles.... I recommend to you the
re-adoption of these valuable little animals is the solution of your difficulties in transporting ore in mountainous places off the railroad where roads are not
passable for wheeled vehicles.*

The burro took another small encore with its work during
the Great Depression. Life was tough for people during those
days, and in some cases the burro literally shared those times
with their human masters. Many out-of-work men, often joined

*The burro "Zeph" was used to help publicize the new Denver to
Chicago Zepher on May 26, 1934.*
Rhoades Photography, Denver Public Library Western
History Department (Rh-1332)

by their wives and children, made a decent living during the Great Depression by panning for gold, working small mines that still had some low grade ore in them, or working the dumps of some of the bigger mines. The ore was so low-grade that this could only be done if costs (and especially the cost of transportation) were kept to an absolute minimum, so often burros were brought back into use. Once again they hauled supplies and brought out ore. These isolated instances of new prospecting and mining were usually successful when done on a small scale, but lasted only until the end of World War II. After that time the burro was again abandoned — this time almost completely.

Of all the "abandoned" burros in Colorado, there is no doubt that "Prunes" of Fairplay is the most famous, although he was not truly abandoned — just left to take care of himself in the winter. Prunes even has a small monument built in his memory. Prunes was not much different from any other burro during the jack's early working days. Prunes was born in 1867 in Buckskin Joe, a town about seven miles north of Fairplay. The burro evidently got his name from his color, which was very close to the color of prunes, and from the texture of his shaggy coat, which was wrinkled like a prune. Yet another version of how Prunes got his name was that it came from his love of dried fruit — especially prunes. Prunes was originally owned by two prospectors, Jack White and Dick Walther. They sold one of their claims to the rich and famous Dolly Varden Mine and in 1889 retired to live out their lives in Denver. Before they left, they took Prunes to Alma, a relatively big town at the time, where they hoped the burro would be easier to sell. They had no problem finding a new master for Prunes — a twenty-nine year old prospector by the name of Rupe Sherwood, who bought Prunes for ten dollars. Rupe was a confirmed bachelor who pretty much stayed to himself, and Prunes became his very dear and trusted friend for life.

Prunes worked hard for Rupe, doing all the work that most burros did for their prospector masters. Rupe eventually staked some pretty good mining claims — the Sherwood being the best. It sold for $15,000. Before Rupe sold the Sherwood Mine, Prunes also worked at many of the local mines when Rupe was trying to make enough cash to buy supplies and head out for another season of prospecting. Because Prunes worked both as a prospector's burro and in the area's mines, he was known to just about everyone in the Fairplay area.

There were even stories told that because Prunes was so well known and so smart he was sometimes sent to town with a shopping list for food and supplies pinned to his pack saddle. The grocer would fill the order, and Prunes would then go back to the mine or to Rupe's camp by himself. Although this tale may not be true, it does show the high degree of trust and regard for Prunes' intelligence held by all the local miners and prospectors. Rupe and Prunes worked together and were close friends for almost forty years. Prunes was then almost sixty years old — an extremely long time for a burro to live.

Rupe did only a little prospecting after World War I, but he kept Prunes, who had by now grown very fond of Rupe's flapjacks. Prunes was now almost sixty years old — an extremely long time for a burro to live. Even though a burro usually keeps its teeth much longer than a horse, by 1929 Prunes was completely toothless, and about all that he could eat was flapjacks (the Western name for pancakes) and biscuits. The townspeople loved Prunes, and when he was in town most of them fed him to the point that the burro was getting fat and spoiled — but Prunes deserved such a life in his old age.

As Rupe got older he did not stay year-round in Fairplay, and he would leave his burro to fend for itself, while he went to Denver for the winter. Prunes would wander around town, taking handouts from the locals and eating garbage from the dump, like most of the other Fairplay burros did. But Prunes was special. He followed a set routine every day, and some people said you could set your clock by where Prunes was along that route. One winter Prunes took refuge in an old shed during a severe storm. The wind blew the shed's door shut, and Prunes was trapped for a week before he was found by some of the town's children, who were worried and went looking for him. Prunes was sixty-three years old by this time, and being locked in the shed with no food or water for days took its toll on him. The old burro was sick and suffering, but somehow Prunes stayed alive until Rupe returned in the spring of 1930. Prunes was just not getting any better, and everyone seemed to agree that he should be put down. Some say Rupe did the dirty work himself, but others said he could not possibly have brought himself to shoot his lifelong friend, so Rupe probably got a friend to do it. Everyone knew that it was the best thing to do so that Prunes no longer had to suffer. For lack of a better place, Prunes' body was taken to the town dump. The well-known burro was sorely missed by all; even the *New York Times* took note of his death.

The Prunes Monument next to the historic Hand Hotel in Fairplay has honored Prunes' memory since 1933.
                                                    Lyn Bezek Photo

All of the local citizens had fallen in love with Prunes, and in 1933 the townspeople raised the money to build a simple monument to Prunes, even though the nation was in the middle of the Great Depression. The five and a half foot tall monument, located on Front Street in Fairplay, reads:

Prunes
A Burro
1867-1930
Fairplay
Alma
All Mines
In This
District

Prune's bones were located at the dump and were buried at the new monument. Rupe wrote a poem for the dedication of the monument. "Me and Prunes" was a ninety-two line piece of poetry that read in part:

So poor old Prunes has cashed it in.
Too bad. Still in a way
I'm glad the old boy's eased off
And calling it a day.... I'm going to miss him scand'lous!
The world won't seem the same,
Not having him a'standing here,
Hee-hawing in the game....

I'm gambling if there is another life after this one,
It won't be just restricted to the thing called man alone,
But everything now living will surely live again —
I know a hundred that deserve to, more than most of men.
An' if they do, why sure as shootin' among those
heavenly tunes
I'll betcha fifty buck we'll hear the hee-haw
of old Prunes.

Prunes' collar and some of his other belongings were put into a glass case built into the monument. Ore from the bigger mines in the area was incorporated into the memorial. Rupe died just a year after the Prunes Memorial was built. He was eighty-one years old and, as requested by him before his death, his ashes were buried next to the bones of Prunes. Today, school children still leave flowers on Prunes' grave, and a number of his offspring still roam the hills around Fairplay. The story of Prunes has even appeared in *Ripley's Believe It or Not*.

There were also a Prunes II, III, and IV. Prunes II (also called Prunes, Jr.) was sent to an Air Force base in Edmonton, Alberta, Canada during World War II. The commanding officer's American wife was assigned the task of choosing a mascot for the base, and she decided that she wanted a "Rocky Mountain burro from her home state of Colorado." The Fairplay Chamber of Commerce found a wild burro and sent it to them. After World War II, Prunes II retired and lived out his life near Calgary, Alberta, Canada. Prunes III was used for fundraising as part of a wartime marketing event and bore a pack load of silver dollars from Fairplay to Denver in 1943 to be given to the the United Service Organization (USO), which helps show support for American soldiers and their loved ones. A ceremony was held at the state capitol building with many dignitaries giving speeches, and Prunes III eventually appeared in *Life* magazine. Prunes IV did the same thing in 1944.

Besides there having been a Prunes II, III, and IV roaming around Fairplay, there was also a follow-up story to Prunes' work in the mines. There was a mine trammer (the man who moves the ore cars) named John Billingsley, who found a substitute burro when Prunes left the Hock Hocking Mine near Fairplay. *The Rocky Mountain News* of July 21, 1949 reported that Billingsley said:

> *Outside of preachers, few now days know that jack-asses chew tobacco. But we of those days knew it.*

Most boys packed a plug. It was a link of sociability.
I chewed Beechnut, a package chew. Some chewed
Horse shoe, Star and others.

   My new jack was a lady. I called her Maudie. Right
off I loved Maudie, and she fell for me like a ton of
slag. The collar and traces irked her a lot. She twisted
and humped showing signs of a balk that stumps a
skinner.

   To seem nonchalant, I pulled my beechnut out.
Maude raised her nose an eighth of an inch.

   I had it. Why hadn't I thought? I peeled back
the package and passed it to her. She nuzzled it a bit
— then she dragged off about twenty cents worth of
my life-giving Beechnut. I loved her some more — and
away we went.

   After that it was Beechnut or no muck (haul ore).
It took a lot of it, but it was worth it to see the boss
beam at me as the jack trainer.

Billingsley later quit working at the Hock Hocking Mine and went to work across the gulch at the Orphan Boy Mine. A few days later he met his former boss in the gulch, who yelled at him, "You have a right to quit and get another job but you ain't got no right to pack away your secret tramming tricks." Billingsley explained the Beechnut treat to his ex-boss, who exclaimed, "The hell, and to think Prunes did it all these years without a chaw."

Almost as famous as Prunes, and with a far more touching story, is that of Shorty, a burro born in 1906, that was so named because he had very short legs, even for a burro. There is a small pink marble stone on the courthouse lawn in Fairplay to memorialize Shorty's life as well as that of his friend Bum. Shorty worked in the mines near Fairplay for a time and was a partner for several prospectors, but he was born just a little too late to have spent much time in the burro's "glory days." Everyone instantly recognized Shorty because of his very short legs. Shorty was good at carrying freight or pulling an ore car, but he did not like to be ridden. As a joke, the men at the mine would always try to get a new man to ride the "gentle, short burro," and the new man would invariably get thrown off. As Shorty got older, he became almost totally blind. The mines were shutting down, and Shorty became the town's beggar. The people of Fairplay loved Shorty just as much as they had loved Prunes. The people of Fairplay understand burros.

Shorty made a friend of a homeless dog named Bum in 1949. Bum had been abandoned as a puppy, and a Fairplay family took the dog in. Bum was part Dalmatian and part something else. Dalmatians were a rare breed in Fairplay, so everyone instantly recognized him. The children of the family loved Bum, but their father evidently mistreated him. One day Bum just walked out of the house and would never go back. It was fall and the nights were beginning to get cold. Only a few days later Bum met Shorty. The dog and the burro curled up next to each other, keeping each other warm during the night. The two hit it off immediately and were always seen together for the rest of their lives.

Somehow Bum knew that Shorty could not see, and the dog took charge of the burro. Lots of burros were guided by dogs in the pack trains, but Bum was never a burro puncher's dog. What happened next utterly amazed the people of Fairplay. Bum and Shorty went begging for food together. They would usually go behind a home or restaurant, and Shorty would bray to let the women know that the two were there. Someone would come out eventually and throw the pair some biscuits or pancakes. Bum would pick up the first few and take them to Shorty to eat. The dog would continue until Shorty had eaten at least half the food, and only then would Bum eat. This happened over and over again at different places around Fairplay, at both breakfast and dinner time. It was not a random event.

When winter came in full force, it got cold — real cold. Bum made friends with Johnny Capelli, the janitor at the local courthouse, who allowed Bum and Shorty to sleep in his garage, even though it meant leaving his car out in the snow. There was no heat, but it was dry and out of the wind. Johnny tried to get Bum to sleep in the house on really cold nights, but Bum wanted to stay in the garage with Shorty. They slept on hay that Johnny spread around in the garage — always curled up together.

In the spring, after breakfast, the pair returned to the nearby hills for the rest of the day, which gave Shorty a chance to eat green grass. At night, after dinner, they would go back to the garage and curl up together again. At breakfast and dinner they were always out begging pancakes, biscuits and other scraps of food from the townspeople. They especially liked to go to the Hand Hotel, where Maggie, the hotel's cook, would feed them special treats. This went on like clockwork for another year. One day in May, Shorty, the blind burro, was hit by a speeding car and died almost instantly. Several people witnessed the car speed off, but Bum was not around. Evidently he was off chasing chipmunks or whatever a dog did on a beautiful spring day in the mountains. Shorty's body was put in a wagon and taken to the city dump. Bum soon showed up looking for Shorty and tracked the burro's body all the way to the dump. Bum sat down by Shorty and would not budge. He kept the magpies and other predators away from his friend's body. When Johnny Capelli heard what had happened, he went to get Bum, but Bum would not leave Shorty. Johnny took food and water to Bum at the dump, but Bum would not eat or drink — the dog was mourning his dead friend.

The next day Johnny went to the dump with a rope, tied it around Bum's neck, and forcibly took Bum back to the garage, where he locked him in. Then he and a few friends went back to the dump and burned Shorty's body. After that Bum never went back to the dump. He became very sad and gloomy, and hung around the garage, and almost never wagged his tail.

Eventually, a monument was placed on the courthouse lawn to commemorate this unusually strong friendship of a burro and a dog. Bum was still alive, so the dog's date of death was left off. There are photographs of Bum sitting next to the new monument. Soon thereafter Bum ran in front of a car and was killed. Some of the townspeople said it was suicide, that the dog wanted to die and could have avoided the car. Johnny took Bum's body to the dump. There he found what he was sure were some of Shorty's bones that had not been consumed in the fire, dug a grave, and put the bodies of the two friends in it, so that they could be together on earth as well as, he hoped, in heaven.

Besides the attachments between burros and dogs, burros also have a very strong attachment to each other. If a close friend or mate of a burro dies, they will almost always go into mourning, and some have even been known to pine away and die. Cotton and Satan were two burros that worked at Seven

The monument to Shorty and Bum still does not have Bum's date of death.

Lyn Bezek Photo

Falls near Colorado Springs. For years they were used for the tourists to ride, and then as they got older they were used like props to allow the tourists to take pictures with them. Cotton was about fifty, when the burro was hit by a large log that rolled down a hill and smashed into Cotton, killing the burro almost instantly. Satan would not leave the spot where his friend had died, and he himself died only one day later.

Perhaps because burros were so abused and so many were killed instead of dying natural deaths, there are many stories of ghost burros. One burro's haunting event happens regularly in Empire, Colorado, where, at dusk (when prospectors and miners would usually be coming home from work), the clip clop of a burro's hooves and his master's footsteps can often be heard on the streets, even though no horse, burro, mule, or human is in sight. The rattle of pots, pans, and other equipment can also be heard. The sounds usually start at the North Empire Mining District, and then go down the main street through town and on to the cemetery on the other side of town, where the sounds fade away. The identities of neither the prospector nor his burro are known.

In the 1870s and 1880s, there were thousands of burros that traveled over the Mosquito Range between Fairplay and Leadville. Many men and burros died on the pass in one of the many horrific snowstorms that could appear very quickly. Several men, including a reporter, have seen an entire ghost burro pack train near the top of the pass. The identity of this group is even known. The burro puncher's name was Caemals and his pack train had about thirty burros in it. Caemals and all his burros froze to death near the top of the pass on a cold winter night when a sudden storm came up and trapped them. On certain nights the burros' ghostly images can be seen moving over the pass with the driver behind his burros, occasionally giving them a sharp rap on the rump when they are going too slow. It would seem that they must have loved their way of life, or maybe they are just trying to finally get over the pass.

A wizened, old prospector and his burros "Rough" and "Ready" were in Boulder, Colorado about 1920.
Parson Photography, Denver Public Library Western History Department (X-60916)

During the years since World War I, there have been times in certain isolated parts of Colorado when more modern forms of transportation have failed and burros and mules have been called to do their freighting job again. This has happened several times along the Denver and Rio Grande Railroad route between Durango and Silverton. Heavy and dangerous snow slides have blocked both the road and the train tracks, leaving mule and burro pack trains to save the citizens of Silverton. The last major blockage of the railroad occurred from December 26, 1951 to March 24, 1952 — a total of eighty-eight days, although the Million Dollar Highway was open during some of that time.

During 1949 and 1950 there was a short revival of interest in burros in Colorado. Politicians took up their cause and announced that statues would be erected and proper recognition given to the small, furry creatures that had played such an important part in Colorado history. Very little action was actually taken, although both *The Denver Post* and *The Rocky*

Mountain News wrote a series of human interest stories about burros and their owners. These interviews were some of the last with those prospectors and burro punchers who had actually lived through the historical experience. The Denver Zoo even located several burros and displayed them for many years. The thought and attention was nice; but a Colorado burro does not belong in a zoo any more than a cow, mule, or horse. Its place is out where its prospector friends would be if still alive, out roaming the valleys and mountains of Colorado; or, if that is not possible, it deserves a good home with a family that will love and care for it.

One of the places in Colorado that continues to take care of its donkeys (they are called donkeys not burros in this community) is the mining town of Cripple Creek. In fact, the eleven basically wild donkeys that currently make up the "world famous" Cripple Creek herd have a very good deal going. The five gelded males and six females have the best of both worlds — they are allowed to roam free and wild much of the year but are also watched over by a lot of townspeople, all of whom have their best interests at heart. Believed to be the descendants of the donkeys that once toiled in the area's many mines, they are protected by city ordinance, given the right-of-way on town streets, and cared for year-round by members of the "Two Mile High Club," who raise money for their hay and veterinary care.

Known as "the world's greatest gold camp," Cripple Creek (where one of the last big gold discoveries was made in Colorado) has been the home of donkeys for 120 years. After gold was discovered there in 1890, hundreds of donkeys were brought to the mines to pack in supplies and bring out the rich ore. Some stayed underground where they worked pulling machinery and ore carts through the tunnels. By the late 1920s, however, the mining of gold began to decline and most of the donkeys found themselves unemployed. As miners left the area to seek their fortune elsewhere, the donkeys were left behind to forage for themselves. Many of them wandered through the hillsides and forests surrounding Cripple Creek and sought no human contact. A group of six to ten of the more sociable donkeys, however, came into town every evening and sidled up in front of the Palace Drug Store to receive handouts from its owner, David Lynch.

About this same time, another businessman in town, Charley Lehew, was trying to come up with an idea that would help attract tourists to the area during the summer. Eventually the two men put their heads together and came up with the idea of a town celebration honoring the donkeys. Along with several other business owners, they formed the Mile High Club, informally adopted the "drug store" herd, and on August 15, 1931, held the first official "Donkey Derby Days." Festivities included a parade with Governor William Adams as the Grand Marshall and riding a donkey, a boxing match, plus people, stock car and

Cripple Creek's donkeys can be found all over town in the summer.
Sandra Haigler Photo

horse races. But the biggest race was reserved for the donkeys. Billed as the "Grand Donkey Sweepstakes Race," the first event attracted thirty-five long-eared entrants and their riders from near and far.

Donkey Derby Days was a big success. With the exception of several years during World War II, the Mile High Club — which eventually changed its name to the "Two Mile High Club" — has continued to sponsor the event every summer. That makes the club one of the oldest non-profit organizations in Colorado. During the mid-1960s, interest in Donkey Derby Days was beginning to diminish. However much-needed enthusiasm was again supplied by a group of Cripple Creek businessmen, who reorganized the Two Mile High Club, built up the donkey herd, and heavily promoted Donkey Derby Days. The date of the celebration was changed from August to the last full weekend in June, where it remains today.

The route of the donkey derby race has evolved and changed over the years. Originally the race was run on a specially-built circular track. It was later changed to a loop from Bennett Avenue uphill to the Molly Kathleen Mine and back. Most recently, it follows a mile-long course around town with stops along the way, where the human participants are required to perform certain miner-related stunts. In years when the city and club come up with attractive prize money, a longer, professional race sanctioned by the Western Pack Burro Ass-ociation, adds to the mix. This race usually starts in the nearby town of Victor, traverses ten miles of mountain trails, and ends in Cripple Creek. Unlike the early years, participants in today's races are not allowed to ride the donkeys because of insurance liability requirements and laws against animal cruelty. They must drag, push, pull, or carry the donkey over the finish line.

A much shorter "Businessman's Race" was added in 1965, and pits local business owners against each other, as they and their donkeys race from one end of Bennett Avenue to the other. Since the advent of gambling in Cripple Creek in 1991, employees of some of the casinos have joined in the fun. This is now the only race that uses the local donkeys. Because the wild donkeys are not halter-trained, some of them never actually finish the race, preferring to go their own way despite their human partner's desires. The winning business goes home with a trophy and bragging rights for a year.

Every year members of the Two Mile High Club volunteer countless hours of their time to make Donkey Derby Days a success. In 2009, the two-day event drew over 50,000 visitors to Cripple Creek. "That's not bad for our little town of 1400," states Bill Loop, the club's Vice President. Proceeds from the sale of tee shirts, caps, donkey books, and toys go directly for the care and feeding of the local donkey herd. The 2009 kid's tee shirt, designed by an eighth grader from Cripple Creek, was so popular it sold out by noon the first day. As another yearly fundraiser, club members conduct Fall Aspen Tours the last two weekends in September, when the hills around the old mining town are ablaze with color. Tour guides share stories of the area's rich mining history and heritage, and all proceeds again go to taking care of the local donkeys.

From April to late October or early November, Cripple Creek's donkeys are free to roam wherever they please. City ordinance limits the herd to a maximum of fifteen and also mandates that all jacks be gelded to minimize aggressive behavior. According to Loop, the herd usually sticks together, staying either in town or within one or two miles of the city limits. While most Cripple Creek residents enjoy the animals and are very protective of them, some consider them a nuisance as they tend to get into trash cans and trample flowerbeds. "You can usually tell where the herd is by following the trail of tipped-over trash cans," laughs Loop.

Even though, from time to time, a few citizens call for moving the donkeys elsewhere, their role as the town's roving ambassadors appears safe. "People can control their trash and fence their yards to protect their flowers — that's part of the responsibility of living in a town with a wild donkey herd," states Tom Cooper, who moved to Cripple Creek from California three years ago and is now the Two Mile High Club's President. "The donkey herd is what Cripple Creek is all about. By working with the donkeys, I feel I'm giving something back to the community."

Tom's wife, Judy, who serves as Secretary of the club, is impressed by how much most of the local residents care about the donkeys. "Many people here treat them like their own pets," she states. Some happily offer them food and some residents put out bird baths, not for the birds but so the donkeys can get a drink. The animals themselves can be quite resourceful and have been known to turn on faucets and unlatch gates with their teeth. In the event of a bad storm, the entire herd will sometimes take refuge in a casino parking garage, which probably provides a surprise for the gamblers that are constantly coming and going.

Melissa Trenary, a Two Mile High Club member and author of *Donkeys of the Gold Camp — An Informative Guide To Cripple Creek's World Famous Donkey Herd*, tells of the time two donkeys banged on her back door, opened the screen door, and came halfway into her kitchen looking for treats.

An informal neighborhood watch system exists to make sure that any donkey having problems gets needed attention right away. A brown and white male donkey named "CoCo" is the reason for many false-alarm calls. He has the habit of lying down on the ground with his legs stretched out and his tongue lolling out of his mouth. The uninitiated think Co-Co is dead and call 911 for help. Sometimes, however, a call of "donkey down" actually portends serious trouble. One cold December day a couple of years ago, a gray jennet named "Flower" was found lying on the frozen ground. The whole community responded and soon blankets, heaters, oxygen, and heat packs had arrived. Volunteers took turns staying with Flower. A local construction company, animal control, the water company, public works, Cripple Creek EMS, and a veterinary clinic all pitched in to help the donkey. Sadly, despite all their efforts, the donkey died from unknown causes.

An incident with another donkey had a happier ending. In the fall of 2009, "Sweet Pea," a dark brown jennet, was observed to be limping and having difficulty keeping her balance. The veterinarian who was summoned found that the donkey had an infected wound in her left flank "consistent with a gunshot wound." A small corral was built for Sweet Pea on property owned by Bronco Billy's Casino so she could rest and be given antibiotics and pain medication. Because donkeys are herd animals and very family-oriented, the other donkeys would come back from their daytime wandering to stay near Sweet Pea at night. She recovered and returned to the herd in early October.

Local news coverage of Sweet Pea's apparent shooting was picked up by the Associated Press and became national news. As a result, the Two Mile High Club received donations for the donkey's medical care from as far away as Kansas and Minnesota. The club has also offered a $500 reward for any information

A wounded Sweet Pea rests in her special "hospital pen" after being shot.

Lyn Bezek Photo

leading to the arrest of the person who shot Sweet Pea. No tips have been immediately forthcoming, but club president Tom Cooper says that he thinks that in time someone will slip up and give himself away. As one Cripple Creek resident was overheard to say, "Nobody better hurt our donkeys — they're sacred!" Jan Collins, Director of the Cripple Creek District Museum, echoes those sentiments. "So many people love the donkeys, and it is terrible to think that someone is messing with them," she says. "It's like slapping your grandma around."

During the time of Sweet Pea's problems, another donkey named "Tarzan" disappeared and there was great concern that Tarzan might have been shot. However, he was found by a rancher about five miles out of town two weeks after his disappearance. The donkey had joined up with a herd of horses that had broken out of their pasture. The townspeople were relieved but not surprised. Tarzan apparently thinks of himself more as a horse than a donkey and has a habit of leaving his donkey herd behind to go play with other equines.

Just like most Americans, donkeys in the Cripple Creek herd struggle with their weight. Although they are wild animals, they are very people-friendly. Tourists delight in feeding them whatever snacks they might have in their cars — pizza, popcorn, chips, sandwiches, etc. — all of which are enthusiastically accepted but are not particularly healthy for the animals to eat. Hay cubes and oat candy, which are more appropriate treats for the donkeys, are for sale at the District Museum Gift Shop. According to Bill Loop, plans are in the works to put donkey food dispensers around town as well as instructional brochures about the proper feeding of the animals. The only other town in the United States to have a wild herd of donkeys is Oatman, Arizona, where shopkeepers sell bags of carrots to tourists who want to feed the hungry critters.

Obesity is an especially dangerous problem for equines due to the possibility of a foot disease called "foundering" or "laminitis." Added weight or too rich a diet can compromise blood flow

The tourists love to feed all kinds of food to the Cripple Creek donkey herd.

Lyn Bezek Photo

to the hooves, leading to tissue death and, in some cases, the death of the animal. To help the local donkeys slim down after they have been overfed by tourists or raided trash cans during the warm weather months, members of the Two Mile High Club — in cars, on foot, and on horseback — round all of the animals up in late October or early November and corral them in their winter pasture on the outskirts of town where their diet can be controlled. There they have shelter, hay, water from a tank that is kept full and ice free by the local fire department, and thirty-acres of pasture in which to roam. While they are confined, a farrier comes several times to trim their hooves, an undertaking which sometimes requires the assistance of three extra people to get the job done. "Donkeys don't much like pedicures," quips Tom Cooper. The herd is released to once again wander on its own when warm weather arrives, usually in April.

Cripple Creek honors its long-eared mascots in many ways. Signs featuring a prospector and his faithful donkey welcome visitors on both main roads leading into town. A bronze sculpture of a jennet and her foal, created by local sculptor Mike Slancik, stands in front of the District Museum. (Knit scarves are wrapped around the necks of both mother and babe during the winter months.) A painted mural of a burro pack train from yesteryear graces the brick wall of Womack's Casino at the corner of Bennett Avenue and Second Street. The Brass Ass Casino, located farther up Bennett Avenue, sells souvenir tee shirts, cups, and pins emblazoned with its golden logo of a donkey. Along U. S. Highway 50 west of Cañon City, a giant billboard featuring a donkey proclaims, "Let's go to Cripple Creek."

In the town of Cripple Creek, "Donkeys At Large" signs warn drivers that the local herd has the right-of-way. One Cripple Creek resident remembers the time years ago when two young foals decided to lie down on their sides and take a nap at the curve of the road near the District Museum. A Cripple Creek

A prospector and his donkey grace Cripple Creek's welcome sign.
Lyn Bezek Photo

The people of Cripple Creek understand donkeys. They have the right of way in their town.

Lyn Bezek Photo

police officer quickly arrived to direct traffic around them while they slept peacefully.

With the arrival of the age of the world-wide web, a short video of the antics of some members of the herd can be viewed on You Tube by googling "Cripple Creek Colorado Donkeys." Their comical trick of sticking their heads through visitors' open car windows, so as to be closer to the food source, is recorded for posterity.

Yes, the people of Cripple Creek love and understand their donkeys. They realize the nobility but vulnerability of the animals, as well as the important role they played in the history of their area.

CHAPTER SEVEN

∞

The Wild Burro
Nuisance or National Treasure?

When they were no longer needed as beasts of burden for prospectors and miners, burros became disposable. Many of them were left to fend for themselves in the mountains and deserts where they had toiled. Adaptable and resilient, feral burros were able to survive fairly easily in the wild. In fact, burros not only survived in the wild, but they quickly multiplied. After the age of three or four, a jennet can produce a foal every twelve to eighteen months for up to thirty years. As a result, wild burro herds can double every four years. As early as the 1920s, concerns were already mounting that there were too many wild burros in the West, and by the last half of the twentieth century, they began to compete with other animals for the limited food supply in their remote home territory. Not only did they forage where deer and bighorn sheep grazed, they often ate grass on leased federal land where local ranchers grazed their income-producing herds of sheep and cattle. Wildlife biologists blamed wild burros for the decimation of many native plants and, as a result, the reduction of some native animal species.

Both ranchers and wildlife experts began to demand that "the burro must go!" Soon it became open season on the long-eared little animals. Some were rounded up and sold as pets, but many more were killed for sport or for commercial purposes (such as being ground up for pet food or fertilizer). Even more animals were simply shot and their bodies left in the desert or remote areas to become food for scavengers, thus being recycled into the environment.

A similar fate was also befalling the wild burro's more glamorous cousin — the wild horse. In the 1950s many Western wild horses were hunted down by "mustangers" to be sold to slaughter houses. The terrified animals were pursued across the prairie by low-flying aircraft until they were near exhaustion. They were then chased by trucks and lassoed with a rope weighted down at the other end with a heavy truck tire. The horses would drag these weights around until they literally dropped. At that point they were hobbled and hauled to a truck where they were packed in like sardines for transport to a slaughter plant.

A young Nevada woman named Velma Johnston happened to be following one of these trucks on her way to work one day and was shocked to see blood dripping from the back of the vehicle. She followed the vehicle to the slaughter house and saw that the blood was coming from injured wild horses. Her outrage spurred her to investigate the cruel manner in which the horses were captured. She courageously documented the round-ups by taking photographs while sitting on the roof of her car. Her husband sat in the car below her with a revolver in his lap.

Velma earned the nickname "Wild Horse Annie," as she drummed up public support to call a halt to these wild horse abuses, and the wild burro was able to tag along in this rescue mission. She spoke to school groups, politicians, businessmen, ranchers, and anyone else who would listen. With her encouragement and guidance, school children and others started a massive letter-writing campaign to Congress on behalf of the horses and burros. An Associated Press news article at the time stated: "Seldom has an issue touched such a responsive chord." Finally on September, 1959, Public Law 86-234 — dubbed the "Wild Horse Annie Act" — was passed, banning air and land vehicles from being used for the purpose of capturing or killing "any wild, unbranded horse, mare, colt, or burro running on public land." The law also banned the polluting of water holes on public land for the purpose of "trapping, killing, wounding, or maiming of the animals." By this time, several western states had already outlawed hunting wild horses and burros by plane on state lands. What the Wild Horse Annie Act did not include, however, was Velma's recommendation that the Federal government begin a program to protect, manage, and control wild horse and burro herds on public lands.

Hollywood kept the issue alive with the 1961 release of "The Misfits," a western starring Clark Gable and Marilyn Monroe. The movie showed a horse round-up near Reno, Nevada, which was portrayed as very troubling to Marilyn Monroe's character in the film. Throughout the 1960s and early 1970s, letters of protest from school children and other Americans continued to flood Congressional offices. On December 15, 1971, these efforts bore fruit when President Richard M. Nixon signed the "Wild and Free-roaming Horses and Burros Act." The Act reads in part:

> Congress finds and declares that wild free-roaming horses and burros are living symbols of the historic and pioneer spirit of the West; that they contribute to the diversity of life forms within the Nation and enrich the lives of the American people; and that these horses and burros are fast disappearing from the American scene. It is the policy of Congress that

> *wild free-roaming horses and burros shall be pro-*
> *tected from capture, branding, harassment, or death;*
> *and to accomplish this they are to be considered in the*
> *area where presently found, as an integral part of the*
> *natural system of the public lands.*

Public lands are defined as lands administered by the Secretary of the Interior through the Bureau of Land Management (BLM) or by the Secretary of Agriculture through the U.S. Forest Service (USFS). (See the Appendix for the entire Act.) After the passage of the Wild and Free-Roaming Horses and Burros Act, the Bureau of Land Management and the U.S. Forest Service became the agencies responsible for protecting, managing and controlling wild horses and burros and their habitat — Wild Horse Annie's key recommendation had finally been signed into law.

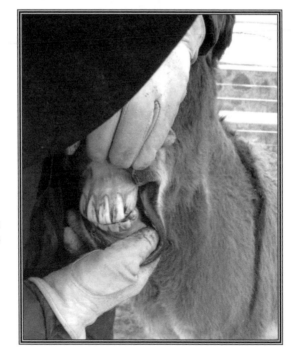

All feral burros get a complete medical checkup, including their teeth.
Lyn Bezek
Photo

Under the 1971 Act, ranchers are banned from killing wild and free-roaming horses and burros, even if the animals are on the ranchers' land; but ranchers can help care for the animals if it is done in a humane manner "that protects them from harassment" and if they are not actually taking wild horses and burros from public land. The government is supposed to be notified if a rancher is taking care of wild animals. No individual is authorized to capture a wild and free-roaming horse or burro for his or her own use — he or she must go through the Bureau of Land Management and U. S. Forest Service programs.

One of the key goals of the Act is to have healthy herds of wild horses and burros thriving on healthy rangelands. To protect the range from deterioration due to overpopulation, it is at times the task of the Bureau of Land Management and the Forest Service to "humanely" capture excess horses and burros and adopt them out to private, qualified individuals through the Wild Horse and Burro Adoption Program. Those animals that cannot be adopted are to be "destroyed in the most humane and cost efficient manner possible." Of those horses and burros that are captured, none can be sold for slaughter for use as pet food or fertilizer.

Safeguarding the health of the wild horse and burro herds as well as the health of the rangeland is often a difficult balancing act and, over the years, the decisions made by the Bureau of Land Management, U. S. Forest Service, as well as the National Park Service (NPS) have often caused controversy. A major upheaval that took place in Grand Canyon National Park focused the national spotlight on the plight of wild burros in a big way.

The Grand Canyon has been home to burros within its towering walls since the days of the conquistadors, when the little animals escaped or were intentionally turned loose. Three centuries later, more burros were brought into the Grand Canyon by Arizona gold prospectors for use as pack animals. When they were no longer needed, they too were let go. They survived and multiplied and, by the time the Grand Canyon was designated a National Park in 1919, wild burros were everywhere. Because they were considered a "nuisance," 2,800 wild burros were killed by National Park Service rangers within the Grand Canyon between 1924 and 1968. The year 1969 turned out to be even more lethal when sharpshooters in military helicopters were brought in to gun down every burro they could find.

As time went on, the rangers, bowing to public outrage at the slaughter of the burros, tried less deadly tactics. Their attempt to simply chase the burros out of the Grand Canyon proved unsuccessful, because many of the animals succeeded in scattering and escaping near the rim. Use of tranquilizer darts proved a failure as well, because burros that were scaling the local cliffs would often fall to their death when the drugs took effect.

By 1976 frustrated National Park Service officials had given up on alternative tactics and announced that the burros would again be hunted and killed. They felt the Grand Canyon burros were not protected under the 1971 Wild Free-roaming Horses and Burros Act because they were "a perceived threat to eco-systems on public lands." But the National Park Service's seek-and-destroy plan was derailed — at least temporarily — for two reasons: 1,400 letters of protest came pouring in from the public and three animal rights organizations — the American Horse Protection Association, the Humane Society of the United States, and the Committee to Save the Grand Canyon Burros — banded together to bring a lawsuit against the National Park Service to prevent the killing. The lawsuit challenged the scientific findings that the wild burros were a threat to other wildlife, claiming instead that the little animals had already evolved over more than a century to fit in with the other species that were native to the Grand Canyon.

The lawsuit ultimately failed, and, in the spring of 1979, the National Park Service was again ready to carry out its burro extermination program, citing an estimated cost of $30,000 to kill the burros versus an estimated cost of $360,000 to capture them. This is when renowned animal rights crusader Cleveland Amory and his organization "Fund for Animals" stepped into the picture. Amory convinced National Park Service officials to let him and his organization try to rescue the burros. Amory's daring plan was to rope the burros, transport them to a corral on the Grand Canyon floor, and then air-lift them, one by one, by helicopter to the rim, using a net sling attached to a fifty-foot cable. Financial and moral support for Amory's proposal came from such celebrities as Princess Grace of Monaco, Angie Dickinson, Glenn Ford, Steve Allen, Mary Tyler Moore, and Burgess Meredith. Under public pressure, the National Park Service gave the Fund for Animals sixty days to round up thirty burros as a trial run.

The operation began on August 9, 1979. Fortunately for the burros, the expert cowboy ropers, cutting horses, herding dogs, and experienced helicopter pilots that Amory hand-picked were up to the task. The most accessible burros were roped first and taken to a newly-built corral to await the helicopter. Later, those animals living deepest in the gorge were rounded up, put on a pontoon boat topped with a plywood corral, and then floated down the Colorado River to a safer spot for airlifting. With each airlift, the helicopter, after reaching the top of the 7,000 foot Grand Canyon walls with its dangling cargo, would lower the burro down gently on its back in the net sling, and then workers would hurry over, untie the sling, and throw the net back inside the helicopter. The chopper then disappeared below the canyon walls to carry out the next rescue. A veterinarian and veterinary students from the University of California at Davis examined each captured burro, which, if found to be healthy, was then released into a nearby corral.

Over the next two years, a total of 575 burros were successfully airlifted out of the Grand Canyon with no injuries to man or beast with the exception of one horse that fell to its death after stepping off a cliff. The cost of the operation was $500,000.

A great deal of the money was donated by the Fund for Animal's 200,000 members.

Some of the rescued burros were adopted by celebrities, as well as other burro enthusiasts, for $400 per animal. Many were taken to the Fund for Animal's newly-purchased Black Beauty Ranch in eastern Texas to await adoption at that location. One little, pregnant jennet with an outgoing personality captured Amory's attention and heart as soon as she was lowered by the helicopter. He named her "Friendly" and took her to the Texas ranch, where she delivered a healthy foal — "Friendly Two"— a few months later. Friendly became Amory's constant companion, always greeting him by shoving her head into his stomach. Thirty years later, Friendly still resides at Black Beauty Ranch, where she now eats a special senior diet, wears a coat in the winter, and enjoys the company of over 300 other burros, some of whom were rescued during later operations at Death Valley

Even captured burros like to push their head into a person's belly.
Lyn Bezek Photo

National Monument and at a naval weapons training center in the Mojave Desert in California. Friendly's benefactor Cleveland Amory died in 1998 at the age of eight-one.

In her biography of Amory, *Making Burros Fly*, author Julie Hoffman Marshall states "the Grand Canyon burro rescue changed not only the way many people would forever view burros, but also the way wildlife would be managed thereafter." The power of public opinion about what should or should not happen on public land had made a difference.

Cleveland Amory had always believed that the National Park Service had a love/hate relationship with the Grand Canyon's burro population. As proof he pointed to the fact that in the 1950s and 1960s, the shelves of the Grand Canyon National Park visitor center's gift shop were stocked with copies of Marguerite Henry's 1951 classic children's book, *Brighty of the Grand Canyon*, which told of the adventures of a little burro that roamed free and wild within the Grand Canyon's walls. Based on a real burro of that name that lived in the Grand Canyon from 1892 to 1922, the story of Brighty was extremely popular with tourists. A statue of Brighty even stood at the entrance of the visitor's center. But in the late 1970s, when the decision was made to shoot the park's burros, both the book and the statue disappeared. Interestingly, after the successful airlift rescue of the burros, copies of "Brighty of the Grand Canyon" once again were stocked in the gift shop.

Over the past three decades, wild horse herds have increased substantially, while the number of wild burros has decreased dramatically. In 1971, when the Wild and Free-roaming Horses and Burros Act was passed, a total of 17,300 horses and 8,045 burros lived on public rangelands in ten Western states. According to Bureau of Land Management statistics, the population of wild horses and burros increase on average at a rate of twenty per cent per year. That rate can be as low as five per cent in years of adverse weather conditions or as high as forty per cent in favorable weather years. The 1971 Act gives the Bureau of Land

Management the responsibility of monitoring rangelands and determining when there are too many wild horses and burros for the land to support (meaning their numbers exceed the limited water and food supply).

Each year excess animals are captured and taken to holding areas to await adoption by the public through the Bureau of Land Management's Wild Horse and Burro Adoption Program. During the early 1980s between 1,500 and 3,000 wild burros were removed from their home on the range each year, but since 2004 that number has dropped to 1,000 or less per year. In 2009, a total of 33,100 wild horses and 3,800 burros roamed public rangelands. This means the number of free-roaming wild horses today is almost double and the number of free-roaming burros is less than half of what it was in 1971. Of the wild burros removed from government land, only about sixty percent are adopted. The rest are sent to public sanctuaries or are "destroyed in the most humane and cost efficient manner possible."

There is still great controversy over what constitutes "detrimental use of the land" by horses and burros or what damage is being done by animals other than horses and burros, like deer and bighorn sheep. There is also a debate over what constitutes "an ecological balance." Even the Forest Service, Bureau of Land Management, and National Park Service disagree. These agencies are directed by law to "consider the recommendations of qualified scientists in the field of biology and ecology" that are outside their agencies, but sometimes the scientists themselves don't agree. To complicate matters even further, the Wild and Free-roaming Horses and Burros Act requires that "the needs of other wildlife species that inhabit the land" be taken into consideration as well, but no specifics are given as to priorities, if any, among the wildlife.

Controversy also surrounds the methods of rounding up or "gathering" the excess wild horses and burros once they are determined to be too numerous. The roundup and capture of wild animals is always stressful to the animals, no matter what the method. In October 1976, Public Law 94-579 — The Federal Land Policy and Management Act — amended the 1971 Act to allow the Secretaries of Interior and Agriculture once again to "contract for the use of helicopters and motorized vehicles to manage wild horses and burros on public lands." The Wild Horse Annie Act of 1959 was, in effect, overturned. In roundups since 1976, hovering helicopters and cowboys on horseback chase the animals toward a trap. Or the animals are trapped by being lured to a certain area using food or water as bait. Once gathered, employees of the Bureau of Land Management must decide which of the wild burros will be suitable for the adoption program and which will be returned to the range. The younger, healthier burros are usually considered more desirable for adoption. Those chosen are transported in trucks to adoption preparation centers.

According to information from the Wild Horse and Burro National Program Office:

> Because recently captured wild horses and burros are very sensitive to people, team members are limited to essential personnel to alleviate stress on the animals. Special attention is given to avoiding loud noise and quick movements by personnel to minimize stress on the animals when they are unloaded at the preparation site.

Once unloaded, the burros are sorted according to age, condition, and sex. Policy states that all animals must receive an examination by a veterinarian within four hours of their arrival. The veterinarian draws blood for the Coggins test to check for Equine Infectious Anemia, administers vaccinations, gives worming medications, and treats any sick or injured animals. Any burro that shows signs of sickness or disease will be separated from the other animals as soon as possible and placed in quarantine. Each animal receives an alpha angle freeze mark on the left side of the neck for future identification and tracking purposes. The freeze mark records the estimated year of birth, the state where the burro was captured, and also four angles that are unique to the animal. Freeze marking is designed to be "an unalterable, permanent, and painless way" to identify the animal.

The burros remain at the preparation facility for a minimum of thirty days to "rest and recover from the stress of the gathering, hauling, and preparation." This also allows them to adjust to domestication, proximity of people, and eating and drinking in captivity. After the thirty days, booster vaccinations are given and the burros are shipped to an adoption site. The animals that are headed to the East, where the adoption demand is often the greatest, will have another rest stop at the Bureau of Land Management's Wild Horse and Burro Holding Facility in Elm Creek, Nebraska before continuing on to their final adoption site. The

The Bureau of Land Management's freeze mark is visible on Radar's neck.

Lyn Bezek Photo

Bureau of Land Management has two kinds of adoption program events: through a permanent holding facility and at a temporary adoption center that is set up only once or twice a year.

The Bureau of Land Management's largest permanent holding facility is 2,500 acres of pastureland east of Cañon City, Colorado, which can accommodate up to 3,000 wild horses and burros. It is one of five holding facilities in the United States that has a Wild Horse Inmate Program (WHIP), in which the nearby Department of Corrections minimum security prisoners help gentle and train seven to ten wild horses each month, plus feed and care for all the other wild horses and burros every day. When the Wild Horse Inmate Program was started in Cañon City in 1986, it was the first program of its kind in the country and dealt mainly with horses.

The dual aims of the Wild Horse Inmate Program are to provide a cost-effective way to train and care for wild horses and burros awaiting adoption and, at the same time, give on-the-job training and teach marketable skills to the inmates for use after their release from prison. Working with the burros and horses can also be very therapeutic for the prisoners, since the animals are non-judgmental, keep the prisoners focused on the present moment, and are known to have a calming effect.

Burros were added to the program at Cañon City in 1995, and today the demand for adoption of burros is about equal to the supply, according to Fran Ackley, Bureau of Land Management Wild Horse and Burro Specialist in Cañon City. "Unlike the wild horses, we have arrived at an ideal herd size of approximately 4,000 free-roaming burros on public lands," he states. "The prisoners usually aren't needed to gentle the burros. Burros are so desirable and readily adoptable that the adopters will gentle them on their own."

To adopt a burro from the Bureau of Land Management, an application must be filled out, outlining what pasture and shelter the adopter can provide for the animal. All applicants must be eighteen years of age or older and cannot have any convictions for inhumane treatment of animals. The cost is $125 for a single burro or $250 for a jennet and her un-weaned foal. Jacks must be gelded. Most of the burros range in age from weanlings to ten years old. Adopters can purchase no more than four animals per year and must sign an agreement that they "have no intent to sell the wild horse or burro for slaughter or bucking stock, or for processing into commercial products, within the meaning of the Wild Free-roaming Horses and Burros Act."

If you adopt a wild burro, the chances are good that you will have to increase the height of the fence around the pasture where you will be keeping the animal. New burro owners are often quite surprised to find out that many burros can jump as high as a horse. Some new owners have their animal "fence broken" by a trainer before bringing them home. To guard against

Radar is always happy to see his old friend Fran Ackley.
Lyn Bezek Photo

inhumane treatment or sale of the animal for slaughter, on-site visits to the adopter's home may be made by the Bureau of Land Management after the adoption, and title to the animal is not given to the adopter until one year has passed from the date of purchase.

Photographs and detailed information on wild burros and horses that are up for adoption can be viewed on the Bureau of Land Management internet auction web page (DOI:BLM Wild Horse and Burro Program). Once the application is approved, animals from the Cañon City facility can be picked up on two designated Fridays per month or the Bureau of Land Management will even pay to have the burro or horse delivered for free if the adopter's home is within 150 miles of Cañon City. In addition to Cañon City, the BLM holds adoptions at different locations throughout the United States and throughout the year. For more information call 866-4MUSTANGS (866-468-7826) or visit wildhorseandburro.blm.gov. As the BLM adoption pamphlet points out:

> *Providing a home for a wild horse or burro is both challenging and rewarding. Adopting a wild horse or burro is a unique opportunity to care for and train a living symbol of our American history.*

Currently there are no officially recognized wild, free-roaming burros on Bureau of Land Management land in Colorado, only wild horses. This is not likely to change in the near future (at least by federal authorities), as wild burros cannot by law be relocated by federal authorities from one area of public land to another, except for removal to specified refuges or for adoptions. Most wild burros and horses live in Arizona — about 12,000 either wild or in sanctuaries. Burros at the Cañon City holding facility come from Nevada, Arizona, and California. At present, according to Ackley, approximately thirty burros are brought to Cañon City for adoption each spring and all get adopted fairly quickly, usually by the fall. Most burros are wanted for pets, some for guard duties, and a few for burro racing. Ackley sometimes takes six or seven of the burros that are up for adoption to the burro races in Fairplay, Leadville, or Buena Vista, where there is always a burro-friendly crowd that might be interested in adopting.

One easy-going and irresistible burro named "Radar," who was captured as a yearling from the Big Bear herd management area in California, will never be adopted. That is because the staff at Cañon City's holding facility refuses to give him up. The burro was given the name "Radar" by Ackley because his floppy ears often point in two different directions, so he will not miss anything. Radar arrived in Cañon City by truck in September, 1996, along with seventy-nine other jack burros. He had been labeled a "problem animal" in the wild because he liked to hang out along the road and shake down tourists for any snack they might be willing to give him. At Cañon City the wild jacks were all penned together and, with the exception of Radar, would get as far away as possible whenever a person would enter the pen. "Radar would bravely depart from his equine buddies and approach anyone who entered the pen, wanting to be petted or scratched," states Ackley. "We decided then and there that Radar wasn't going anywhere, certainly not to some far-off state where we wouldn't know his fate. You might say he adopted us. He has been the wild burro mascot for Colorado ever since."

Ackley began training Radar shortly after his arrival at Cañon City. The burro was very agreeable to most things, but like many of his species, did not much like crossing any body of water and preferred not to walk into a trailer. "We would take him on trail rides with us, checking fence or livestock, where he had no choice but to follow or be left behind," states Ackley. "He always followed, but if we got out of sight he would bray and expect us to come back and coax him along (which we did)."

Because Radar is the poster burro at Bureau of Land Management adoptions, at parades and other civic events, a pack saddle and panniers (side baskets) were custom-made for the burro. With his panniers filled with BLM posters and brochures, he is a walking public relations agent and always proves to be a people-magnet. Radar was featured one year in the parade at Donkey Derby Days in Cripple Creek and his picture was used in the Royal Gorge area tourist guide. The burro's fame has spread to local newspapers, according to Ackley, where the typical photo "contains his mug looking straight into the camera and filling up the frame." Radar also makes appearances at local public schools to teach children about the history of the Wild Horse and Burro Program, and he lets the kids ride and climb on him, seemingly unperturbed by his rock star status and all the attention he inevitably receives. Ackley states:

Radar's big mug fills up the frame of many local newspaper photos.
Lyn Bezek Photo

*Radar will be part of Colorado's Wild Horse and Burro
Program for a long time to come. He earns his keep
by being friendly and showing adopters what to look
forward to if they adopt a burro. For this reason, he is
responsible for the adoption of many burros in Colorado. We could not ask for a better ambassador.*

In 2006 Radar was inducted into the Wild Horse and Burro
Hall of Fame, for which he received an official plaque. Even the
warden of the prison has fallen under Radar's spell. He always
includes the burro on the tours he gives of the holding facility
and never forgets to bring him an apple.

Although the Cañon City holding facility is the most cost-
effective in the country, the overall budget for the Bureau of
Land Management to maintain wild horses and burros on public land and to also care for those in holding areas rises every
year. The cost to taxpayers under the Wild and Free-roaming
Horses and Burros Act rose from $39.2 million in 2007 to $63.9
million in 2010. A suggestion by Bureau of Land Management
officials in 2008 that they might turn to euthanasia to reduce
the horse and burro herds caused an immediate and loud outcry
from horse and burro lovers, animal advocates, and members
of Congress. The only alternatives seem to be the expenditure
of more taxpayer dollars as the herds grow, an increase in adoptions (which actually were down in 2009 due to the economy),
or improved fertility control measures.

In October, 2009, Secretary of Interior Ken Salazar — a
Colorado native from the San Luis Valley — proposed several
actions "aimed at protecting the horses, the public lands, and
the taxpayers." He called for the purchase of new public pre-
serves in the Midwest and East at a one time cost of $42.5 mil-
lion to provide sanctuaries for the animals. The idea is to move
some of the burros and horses to land that has not been subject
to years of drought and wildfires as much land in the West has
been. This action might also be a way to more easily share these

Radar likes to hang around with his horse buddy "Skipper."
Lyn Bezek Photo

wonderful animals with other parts of the country. But there are those who say wild burros and horses should stay in the West, where they symbolize the freedom of the American spirit.

Secretary Salazar also believes the government should seek to better control the reproduction rate of the animals through sterilization and contraception with the ultimate goal of the birth rate eventually equaling the adoption rate. Currently, fertility control methods are only ninety per cent effective and last only one year, but the Bureau of Land Management is partnering with the Humane Society of the United States to develop birth control that is more effective and lasts for several years. This seems to be one part of the problem upon which government agencies and animal advocates can agree. The overpopulation of any animal species can only ultimately be solved by getting to the root of the problem and preventing an exploding birth rate in the first place.

In an opinion column written by Secretary Salazar that appeared in the *Los Angeles Times* on January 14, 2010, he called

for a "comprehensive and balanced approach built on new part-
nerships, new thinking and new courage to tackle an issue that,
unfortunately, has no easy solution." He stated that the federal
government alone cannot restore the health of wild herds:

> *We need citizens to help. We want Americans to visit*
> *their public lands where horses (and burros) roam, to*
> *help us care for these magnificent animals, to share*
> *their ideas with us and to help us find citizens and*
> *animal lovers across the country who will adopt wild*
> *horses (and burros) and provide healthy, happy homes*
> *for them.*

The Bureau of Land Management is charged by federal law
to sell "without limitation" (in other words, animals could be
put down or go to slaughter houses) any animal over ten years
old (a youngster for a burro, but middle-age for a horse) or any
animal that has been passed over three times for adoption.
However the Bureau of Land Management has so far made
it its policy to not knowingly sell to a slaughter house or to a
"killer buyer" who might send the animals to a slaughter house
in another country.

Because the wild burro problem (as opposed to the wild
horse problem) seems to be pretty much under control, any new
provisions to the Wild and Free-roaming Horses and Burros
Act would affect the current exploding wild horse population
of 33,000 far more than the fairly stable wild burro population
of 4,000. And in an October, 2009 teleconference, the Secretary
specifically said that his proposals will not have any effect on
the Cañon City holding facility. "What they are doing in Cañon
City works very well," he stated. However, one thing is certain
— there will continue to be controversy about how the Bureau of
Land Management, United States Forest Service, and National
Park Service carry out their responsibilities to the wild herds
and the public rangelands. Critics want the round-ups of excess

animals stopped because they say the collection process is too stressful and dangerous for wild equines, sometimes resulting in injuries such as broken legs, broken necks, and spontaneous abortions. They also accuse the Bureau of Land Management of "wildly" overestimating the number of wild horses and burros on the range and want an independent count made by a non-governmental source.

The Bureau of Land Management asserts that without the intervention of removing excess animals, "many burros and horses would die a slow and cruel death from starvation and dehydration." Cattle and sheep ranchers who lease public land from the Bureau of Land Management and the United States Forest Service continue to complain that wild burros and horses are competing unfairly with their sheep and cattle for scarce food and water, and therefore should be removed. Animal welfare groups continue to claim that sheep and cattle grazing should be curtailed on public land so that our national treasures — wild horses and burros — can thrive on the land that has rightfully been set aside for them.

This very emotional battle has been going on openly and behind the scenes for forty years, and it will likely continue well into the foreseeable future. At least there is a renewed national spotlight focused on the welfare of the wild herds and a begrudging acknowledgment from all sides that there are no easy solutions. As Curtis Imrie, who has probably been the Bureau of Land Management's most frequent burro adopter through the years, has pointed out: "It's fashionable to knock the government, but they certainly do a better job distributing burros than the 'Mustangers' and the rendering plants did in the decades before Congress acted." Amen to that statement.

CHAPTER EIGHT

∽∾

Burro Racing
A Unique Colorado Sport

Every summer for the past six decades, the sounds of burros braying, humans grunting and panting, and crowds cheering have echoed through the Rocky Mountains as Colorado's indigenous sport of burro racing pits man, woman, and beast against truly treacherous terrain. The burros and their human partners run at high elevations, sometimes above timberline, through icy creeks, and across boulder fields. They can encounter all kinds of weather — from heat to rain to sleet to snow — sometimes all in the course of one race.

On July 30, 1949, the first official Rocky Mountain Pack Burro Championship Race started in Leadville, Colorado, followed the twenty-three-mile "Old Stage and Toll Road" over 13,182 foot Mosquito Pass, and ended in Fairplay, Colorado. The racers and their burros, generally from nearby mining towns, had trained for months. Ed Knizely of Fairplay and his burro "Prunes IV" were the local favorites. Their popularity was severely challenged by Melville Sutton, a miner from nearby Como, and his burro "Whitey." Eventually Sutton and Whitey won the race with the time of five hours, ten minutes, and 41.2 seconds. Knizely and Prunes IV came in second. Of the twenty-one runners who started the race, only thirteen finished.

Some say the idea for the very first burro race came about over 100 years ago when two Colorado prospectors struck gold at the same place and raced with their loaded-down burros to town to officially file their claim with the local recorder. Since their burros were loaded with provisions, the prospectors had to run alongside. Others say the idea for the race had its inception with a bet between drunken miners at a Leadville drinking establishment. In reality, the idea was the brainchild of civic-minded Chamber of Commerce leaders in Fairplay who wanted to come up with an event that would honor the mining region's burros and prospectors and add some money to the town's coffers at the same time.

Initially, burro racing was intended to be a "men-only" sport and, to that end, had a rule that all of the human participants had to have a beard to enter. That did not stop the ingenious Edna Miller of Alma, however. She ran with her burro "Pill" in 1951, and another burro, "Nugget," in 1953. To get around the beard requirement, she fashioned one for herself out of hair from her burro's tail. The first official women's division of the burro race appeared in 1955. Stella Smith of Rosita and her burro "Jackie" beat nine other female entrants to capture the title.

By this time burro racing was receiving national attention on Dave Garroway's "Today" show and on national sports shows. The 1955 race was the first one won by Joe Glavinick of Leadville. It was obvious that he had a special rapport with his burros, which kept him winning for over twenty years. In the 1960s, Glavinick's races against marathoner Steve Matthews became legendary and proved that it takes more than being a good long distance runner to win a burro race. Most successful racers train with their burro for months ahead of time so that they can establish a rapport with the animal before the race begins.

Glavinick was the last true miner to run in the race, and he beat several Olympic marathon hopefuls. During the 1970s, with the winding down of the local mining industry, a new crop of racers emerged in large part due to Lee Courkamp, a cross country coach from Arvada, Colorado. He persuaded his high school teams to train with a group of seasoned burros, an unconventional idea which apparently paid off when his teams went on to win several state championships. The coach also was instrumental in the career of Olympic runner Jon Sinclair, who won the Fairplay burro race in 1977.

The route of the burro race remained the same for the first four years. Then, in 1953 and for the next sixteen years, the starting place of the race alternated between Leadville and Fairplay. This was done for the sake of fairness, since most tourist dollars were spent in the town where the race ended.

To drum up national exposure for the annual burro race, in 1953 two Leadville miners, Andy Anderson and Mac Mapin, and a burro named "Roscoe" took the train to California and walked 1,400 miles back to Leadville. As they plodded along the byways of California, Arizona, New Mexico, and Colorado, the men contacted the newspaper in each town for some free publicity and also sent bulletins about their progress to the *Rocky Mountain News* in Denver, which was a co-sponsor of the race.

The race in 1959 proved to be a particularly exciting one as miner Joe Glavinick and his burro "Bon Bon" managed to turn in a record time despite starting out in a driving rainstorm in Fairplay and encountering snow at the top of Mosquito Pass. According to the Leadville newspaper, *The Herald Democrat*, a crowd of 30,000 people cheered as the pair crossed the finish line in Leadville. Glavinick, who loved and respected his burros, declared he would use the $700 prize money to buy oats for Bon Bon. Over the next seventeen years, Glavinick would go on to win eight more times with two different burros, "Pill" and "Ringo."

By the late 1960s friction started occurring between the towns of Leadville and Fairplay, which led in the early 1970s to each town establishing its own race. Leadville designed a twenty-two-mile course which became known as the "Leadville International Pack Burro Race." The route started at the Lake County court house in Leadville, went to the top of Mosquito Pass, then back down the pass, returning to town through California Gulch. Fairplay experimented for a couple of years with a route from Breckenridge over Hoosier Pass to Fairplay and one from Fairplay through Placer Valley to Quartzville and back. Then in 1973, Fairplay settled on a twenty-nine mile course to the top of Mosquito Pass through a tundra field called American Flats and back to the finish line at the Prunes Monument in Fairplay. Because racers must negotiate a vertical gain of more than 3,000 feet, Fairplay's newly-named "World Championship Pack Burro Race" was touted as the planet's "longest, highest, roughest, and toughest race." Eventually, both of the towns developed shorter courses of fifteen miles as well.

The racers (human and animal) take off from the starting line at the Buena Vista race.

Lyn Bezek Photo

Over the years, common rules for the races have been established by the Western Pack Burro Ass-ociation (WPBA), which was formed to promote the sport of burro racing. (See Appendix B) WPBA's website proclaims:

> *We're a bunch of sometimes goofy individuals who love the outdoors, adventure, physical challenges, our burros, and having a good time with the seemingly improbable sport of burro racing.*

To honor Colorado's mining heritage, from a time when prospectors walked beside their loaded-down burros, the rules state that racers must use a rope, attached to their burro's regulation halter, that is no more than fifteen-feet long. All burros in a race must carry a pack saddle with a gold pan, pick, and shovel, weighing a minimum of thirty-three pounds. Water, food, and clothing used during the race are not considered to be part of the minimum weight requirement. The weight is checked at the beginning and finish of the race. Burros may not carry the human, but the human partner, using his fifteen-foot lead rope, may push, pull, drag, or carry the burro. It is the burro's nose crossing the finish line that determines the winner.

Many runners describe the equine-handling skills required in the race as an art form. The human and burro must stay together during the race, although either one may be in the lead. They need to be able to work very closely together with neither being the "boss." The burro is being asked to do something it normally does not do — run for miles at a time in the mountains. It is up to the human to convince his or her burro that all this running up and down the mountains is actually a swell idea. Burro racer Dave TenEyck of Leadville puts it this way: "Burro racing is a partnership, but it is not an equal partnership. The burro weighs up to 850 pounds. It has full veto power."

Runners must keep full control of their animals at all times. This is especially true for participants racing with a jack. Any burro that interferes with another runner or burro can be disqualified. Cruelty is not tolerated and any racer mistreating his or her burro can be disqualified. Race officials have the right to hold a winning burro for up to thirty minutes after a race so that the animal can be examined by a veterinarian to make sure that it has not been mistreated.

In 1978 — the year that Affirmed won the Triple Crown of horse racing — a third race was added in the nearby mountain town of Buena Vista, so that burro racing could have its own Triple Crown. The Fairplay race is usually held in late July and is twenty-nine miles for the men and fifteen for the women. Leadville's course is twenty-two miles for the men and fifteen for the women and is held in early August. The twelve-mile Buena Vista Race is held a week before or after the Leadville race. These three races make up what is sometimes known as "the poor man's Triple Crown" due to the small amount of prize money compared to the lucrative purses in horse racing. The Buena Vista course crosses the suspension bridge over the Arkansas River and traverses the Whipple Trail to the Midland Railroad grade. No additional shorter or longer race course has been added in Buena Vista.

Any man who wins the two long races plus the Buena Vista race and any woman who wins the two short races plus the one at Buena Vista receives the Triple Crown trophy and additional prize money. The winner must have partnered with the same burro in all three races. Since the three events are held on consecutive weekends, participants who run in all three races do so within the space of fifteen days. That allows for very little time between contests for humans and burros to rest their feet and hooves.

Over the years there has been no one male racer that has repeatedly won the men's division of the Triple Crown, but one female racer certainly has dominated the women's division. Since she started racing in 1991, Barb Dolan of Twin Lakes has won the Triple Crown trophy an impressive eleven times

Bobby Lewis and his burro Wellstone cross the finish line to win the 2009 Fairplay burro race.

Lyn Bezek Photo

with three different burros — "Sailor", "Chugs", and "Dakota." Dolan, also a former ultradistance runner, swimmer, and competitive cyclist, was inducted into the Colorado Sportswomen Hall of Fame.

Some races can be incredibly close. With no photo finish technology or instant replays available, a tie is sometimes declared and the prize money is then divided equally by the two contestants. A tie occurred at the 2005 Buena Vista race between Bobby Lewis of Buena Vista and his burro "Wellstone" and Barb Dolan and her burro Chugs. In 2009, Bobby Lewis, again with Wellstone, edged out veteran racer Hal Walter of Westcliffe and his burro "Laredo" by a mere two seconds in both Fairplay and Buena Vista and by nineteen seconds in Leadville to win the Triple Crown trophy.

What explains such close finishes — literally tying, losing, or winning by a nose — after traversing so many miles?

Hal Walter, who has been a regular on the burro racing circuit for thirty years, says the explanation might be that there is a dynamic going on between the burros that only they know about. His running partner Laredo, who is Wellstone's father, just would not go past Wellstone at the finish line at any of the three 2009 races. "I think maybe I'll run with a different burro next year," he laughs.

"Burros like to buddy up and run in tandem," according to veteran racer Curtis Imrie of Buena Vista, who is sometimes called the "Iron Man of Burro Racing," because he hasn't missed a racing season since 1973. "It's really a burro race, not a people race."

Dave TenEyck, who has been racing for twenty years, agrees that the burro — who he calls "the thinking man's equine"— really has the control in the partnership. "They must know and trust you in order to race. They think a lot and you must learn to think like them and anticipate what they are going to do next." He says he gets bored with straight running. "Running with a burro is much more interesting."

The challenge of developing a rapport with his burros is what keeps another long-time racer, Bill Lee of Idaho Springs, coming back for more. "It's the camaraderie of being with an animal out in beautiful mountain scenery that keeps me hooked on burro racing."

Barb Dolan, known for her fabulous way with burros and also her gracious sense of sportsmanship with the other human racers, says she trains a new animal by first observing the way it communicates with its tail, eyes, and ears. "Burros are sweet, have big hearts, and are willing to please. Once you form a bond with them, they're great." She states she is the only one who can manage and run with her spunky burro Chugs. "I just like the attraction of running with an animal, and I like taking care of the animals every day."

All sorts of burros are entered in today's races — wild, domesticated, jacks, geldings (castrated males), jennets, and even miniatures. A wild burro has a "vitality" that is missing in a domesticated animal, according to Curtis Imrie, who has adopted many wild burros from the Bureau of Land Management over the years. Jacks, in general, are more aggressive and have more endurance. Geldings are more manageable. Jennets, although smaller and maybe not as strong, can sometimes have more heart. "Boogie," one of Curtis Imrie's jennets, was the first female burro to win the Leadville race. Dave TenEyck had racing success with a little female named "Matchless," who got her name from being born inside the famous Matchless Mine in Leadville. "She won the Buena Vista race one year," says Ten Eyck. "She never won either of the long races, but she always had the heart to finish." Miniature burros also usually lack the stamina to win the long races, but can do well in the short races, according to Ralph Herzog of Fairplay, a racer since 1982, who races with his miniature burro "Ruby."

Burros in the race sometimes balk or veer off the course. They can buck, bite, kick, and break away from their runners. If the burro and the runner separate, they have to go back to

A young foal stays close to its mother at Curtis Imrie's ranch. Note the cross on the foal's back.

Lyn Bezek Photo

the point where they separated or they are disqualified. These "unknown factors" can play a very important part in the race. Many burro racers do not lead their burros, but rather they jog back by the burros' hips. Burros do not respond well to being led and dislike being pulled even more, so burro racers usually use voice commands that the burro may or may not follow, depending on its mood. Another factor that also needs to be figured into the equation is that the burro needs time to think about all this.

Dave TenEyck calls burro racing "fast, furious, wild, and dangerous." The potential for injuries — for both human and burro — is very real. Back in 1954, during a practice run the day before a race, an uncooperative burro named "Kingo" dragged his racing partner John Stuart over boulders for almost half a mile. Bruised and bandaged, Stuart showed up at the starting line the next day with Kingo, ready to race. History repeated itself as the cantankerous Kingo proceeded to fight Stuart every step of the way. The two took turns dragging each other along the course and, in either an amazing show of determination or insanity, both finally staggered over the finish line more than four hours after everyone else had gone home. Another time, a man finished the race with a collapsed lung thanks to a kick in the chest from his burro. And another runner was nearly dragged to his death by his burro in the early 1980s. One young burro died, most likely of dehydration, soon after finishing the race in the mid-1980s.

Because of the injury potential, checkpoints manned by ham radio operators are set up along the race routes. The radio operators can call for medical help if needed and also communicate the progress of the runners to officials back at the finish line. Water and words of encouragement are also offered to the racers at each checkpoint.

No whips, clubs, or electric prods are allowed. Some runners actually tie the end of the fifteen –foot rope around their waists and allow their burros to pull them. Each runner and burro team has its own style. Only regular training lets them discover exactly what that style is. In training sessions they will try to cross creeks, run on asphalt, run where there is noise or a lot of people, cross bridges, and go across very rocky areas — all things that they will probably face during a race. Barb Dolan states:

> *Burro racing is more like surfing than running. Running is all about control.... Burro racing is like catching a good wave. Natural forces larger than you are at work (that's the burro she is talking about). You just need the knowledge and focus to latch on when the right moment comes.*

As with the burros, all sorts of people enter burro races today — wild, domesticated, males, females, all sizes and ages, and from all walks of life. The ones who keep at it seem to have three things in common — unbridled enthusiasm for the sport, love and respect for their shaggy partners, and a thorough appreciation of the achingly beautiful mountain scenery where the races take place.

Even though Colorado's high country weather limits burro racing to the summer months, training for both human and burro may go on almost year-round. Curtis Imrie and Barb Dolan give their burros some rest and relaxation during the winter months. "My burros hate ice," states Dolan. "They know that running on ice is treacherous." Other racers like Dave Ten Eyck and Bill Lee say they start training for the next year as soon as the summer's races are over.

For those who are just starting out in burro racing, three much shorter and more laid-back races have been organized in recent years at Georgetown, Idaho Springs, and Cripple Creek. They can be good testing grounds before tackling the longer Triple Crown races. The Georgetown race is an eight-mile loop to Empire and back. The Idaho Springs race is just four miles long but includes steep climbs and a lot of switchbacks. It traverses the ominous-sounding "Oh My Gawd Road." Cripple Creek's Donkey Derby Race (which is not sanctioned by The Western Pack Burro Ass-ociation) is a combination of a one-mile race and various "events" along the way that tie into the old-time prospecting days. Halter-trained donkeys are brought in for the race and are not part of the wild herd at Cripple Creek. The schedule for all the official races can be found at

The World Championship Pack Burro Racing Winner's Monument stands next to the Prunes' Monument in Fairplay.
Lyn Bezek
Photo

www.packburroracing.com. Usually burro races are part of each town's summer celebration: Burro Days in Fairplay, Gold Rush Days in Buena Vista, Boom Days in Leadville, Railroad and Mining Days in Georgetown, Tommyknocker Days in Idaho Springs, and Donkey Derby Days in Cripple Creek.

Through the years, other Colorado towns have held burro races — Antonito, Blackhawk, Breckenridge, Central City, Colorado City, Copper Mountain, Dillon, Eagle, Frisco, Golden, Lake Vallecito, Salida, and Westcliffe — but they did not turn into annual events. Two out-of-state races also took place, one in Chama, New Mexico and one in Safford, Arizona. But it is in the central Colorado towns of Leadville, Fairplay, and Buena Vista where folks have managed to keep the spirit and tradition of burro racing alive and well for years.

In 2000, to honor all the winning human-burro teams of the last fifty years, the Western Pack Burro Ass-ociation erected a World Championship Winner's Monument on Front Street in Fairplay — right next to the Prunes Monument. With a hopeful nod to the future, fifty additional brass plaques were included to honor the next half century of winners.

Ardel Boes, a Colorado School of Mines math professor (the school's mascot is the burro), has won the Fairplay race seven times and was the first racer to break the four-hour barrier for the twenty-nine mile course, a feat that was thought to be as impossible as the four-minute mile. Tom Sobal of Salida and his burro Maynard still hold the Fairplay long course record at three hours, forty-four minutes, and eighteen seconds, a record they set back in 1989. In 2009, Dale and Kathy Fitting, owners of the Hand Hotel, instituted a special prize — the Champion's Challenge — which awards an additional $500 if the Fairplay long course winning team breaks the record time of Sobal and Maynard. The amount of $500 will be added yearly until the all-time record is finally broken. They also instituted another prize of $500, which will be awarded if the long course winner beats the previous year's winning time (but not the all-time record). This prize money will also accumulate each year until the prize is won.

In 2007 a campaign was started to request the Colorado General Assembly to designate burro racing as the official state sport. The idea originated with the students at Edith Teter Elementary School in Fairplay (their mascot is also the burro) and was soon backed by the Western Pack Burro Association. An online petition made the case for burro racing by lauding it as the state's only indigenous sport and pointing out that burros "are living history and connect people to the historic heritage of Colorado."

A setback seemed to occur in March of 2008 when the General Assembly voted to designate skiing and snowboarding as Colorado's official winter recreational sports. But the campaign is not dead, according to WPBA Media Relations Director Brad Wann of Highlands Ranch. He reasons that Colorado has three official rocks, so therefore should be able to have more than one official sport. "We're doing a full court press at the Legislature and I think that a vote in favor of burro racing will happen this year (2010)."

Ed Quillen, a freelance writer and publisher of *Colorado Central Magazine*, wrote in a *Denver Post* article in August, 2008:

> *Granted, in the whole world, there are probably fewer than 1,000 people who have ever competed in a pack-burro race. But the sport was born here and continues here. Shouldn't it be quality and a sense of place, rather than popularity and marketing that determines our official state sport?*

As for sense of place, Mosquito Pass may not be as glamorous or as famous (or as accessible) as some of Colorado's well-known ski mountains like Breckenridge or Vail or Aspen, but the lofty peak has seen an incredible amount of history in the making. This is where pack burro teams battled through blinding blizzards and wicked windstorms to keep some of the richest gold and silver mines in the world going full-tilt. This is where stagecoaches and wagons careened their way along a rocky trail, carrying newcomers with dreams of a new life on a new frontier. This is where Methodist preacher Father John Dyer, even well into his seventies, crossed back and forth countless times on skis or snowshoes to deliver mail and the word of God to the rough and tumble mining camps of Fairplay, Alma, and Leadville. It seems fitting that in both the Leadville and Fairplay burro races, the Father Dyer Memorial at the summit of Mosquito Pass is the turn-around point where the runners head back down. If Father Dyer had been alive today instead of back in the 1860s, he probably could have given present-day racers a run for their money.

And then there is the sense of culture that is wrapped up in the sport of burro racing. Curtis Imrie calls it the "western-ness" of the race. "Welcome to the secret Colorado — the last of the true West," he writes in his yearly *Calendar & Ass-ays*.

> *The first four miles of any burro race are as exciting as Teddy Roosevelt's charge up San Juan Hill with the Rough Riders; and the last mile of any burro race is as tough as anything we'll ever do. These are knights and foot soldiers out there, only more democratic. The runner works as hard as the burro. That's why we bond so strongly with our burros. Teachers, mothers, politicians, merchants, miners, writers, unemployed, dentists, artists, students, lawyers, clerks. They're here to dance with the understanding of courage, the joy of play, demonstrate their animal management skills, look chance in the eye, be involved with nature and maybe learn a little something about the significance of survival in the western arena. Lofty stuff for such an egalitarian sport.*

Considering the grueling nature of burro racing and the sheer grit and athletic ability required from all of its competitors, the sport does not seem to garner the respect and attention it deserves. The reason may lie in the fact that only those directly involved in it truly know what is involved. When the gun sounds at the beginning of a race, those of us on the sidelines watch the human-burro teams all take off together in a stampede of dust and noise (burros have a pack mentality so when one gets moving, they all get moving). Then hours later we see each team, caked with dirt and sweat, straggle in and cross the finish line. What we do not see is what each human and burro has endured and conquered during those hours they were away. Burro racer Hal Walter, who is a free lance writer and author of the book, "Pack Burro Stories," puts it this way:

> What the spectator has no clue about is distance, vertical gain, burro-handling, and mountaineering. You hear very little about pack-burro racing, but the sport demands a high level of fitness from both human and beast, as well as some peculiar talents. These animals see little glory in running 20 to 30 miles and require skilled persuasion to get them over a course.

At least in burro racing the partnership between human and burro is fairly equitable. Unlike in the old mining days when the burro definitely got the short end of the stick, the human racers have to work as hard as the burros do, with the exception of the thirty-three pound load of gear the animal is required to carry in the race. But thirty- three pounds for a burro is pretty much a drop in the bucket — or gold pan.

Brad Wann, a newcomer to burro racing with just one season of racing under his belt, describes his experience with the sport as "life-changing." He recently bought two burros in Wyoming and says that his wife and two oldest children are also interested in racing. Relative newcomers Bobby Lewis and

Karen Thorpe were both Triple Crown winners in 2009 and represent new blood in the sport. The 2009 Fairplay race had a record number of thirty-four entrants, which bodes well for the future of burro racing.

As for most of the veteran racers, no one seems to have any plans of retiring anytime soon. For them the journey appears to be just as important as the destination. Curtis Imrie remarks that "my burros ensure that I'm going to use my body in the great outdoors up and down Mosquito Pass until I have to crawl." Hal Walter is philosophical about the future of the sport. "Burro racing may fade into the history from which it was born. Or it may live on as the only sport indigenous to Colorado. Whatever happens in this crazy sport, I'm glad to have been along for the run."

It is not the prize money that keeps them coming back year after year. It is the challenge of partnering with another creature to accomplish something that few of us on the sidelines could ever do. Hopefully, runners will line up for many more years to come and "Get Their Ass Up the Pass."

Burro racers take off down Harrison Avenue during the start of the Leadville burro race.

Lyn Bezek Photo

CHAPTER NINE

୭୦୦

Donkey Rescue
Getting a Second Chance

Fortunately for the many forgotten, neglected, and abused burros of Colorado (or donkeys as we will label them in this chapter) Kathy Dean of Bennett, Colorado, decided in 1999 to establish a shelter exclusively for homeless donkeys. The idea came to her when she found out that almost all of the local horse rescue shelters were focusing only on horses. She discovered that many unwanted donkeys were brought to sales barns and quickly shuttled off for slaughter. Wanting to provide an alternative to the slaughter house, she knew she would need to provide a facility where the animals could be rehabilitated and trained while a new owner was being found.

About that same time, she met three other women who were crazy about donkeys. Each woman had a different and essential skill to offer. So one day Dean bought five emaciated, beaten-up, and beaten-down donkeys that were about to be shipped to a slaughterhouse. She took them home to her twenty-acre ranch

*Longhopes Donkey Shelter Executive Director Kathy Dean poses
with "Sugar."*

Longhopes Donkey Shelter Photo

in Bennett, a rural area twenty miles east of Denver, to join her
three other donkeys, one of which was a forty-two-year-old animal that she had recently taken in.

Even though she admits she did not know much about
donkeys, suddenly she had gone from having three to eight.
"I fell in love with them," she says. "And I feel strongly that if
you have everything you need in your own life, it's up to you
to do charity work. Saving donkeys turned out to be my passion." The end result was Longhopes Donkey Shelter, which is
a non-profit organization "dedicated to the rescue, rehabilitation, shelter and re-homing of abandoned donkeys." It is the
only shelter exclusively for donkeys in the Rocky Mountain
Region.

Some donkeys arrive at the shelter because their owners are no longer willing or able to care for them. Others are confiscated from their owners by authorities due to abuse or severe neglect. Neglect of any type can result in thin and unhealthy animals that may be starving and also may have psychological problems because of the abuse. As a result, their hair sometimes is falling out, and many of the jennets are also pregnant — adding to the emotional and physical strain they already have on their bodies.

One of the most common physical problems seen in rescued donkeys is overgrown hooves, some to the point that the animal can barely walk. Hoof trimming ideally should be done three to four times a year. At a cost of thirty to fifty dollars per trim, many owners are unwilling or unable to keep up with

The front hooves of the donkey at the left and all four hooves of the donkey at the right are terribly overgrown.
Longhopes Donkey Shelter Photo

*Two of the
rescued
Longhopes
donkeys "dancing
cheek to cheek."*
Pamela Moser
Photo

this very necessary care, or they live where there are no professional hoof trimmers (farriers), or an owner may have spent
so little time with their donkey that it will not stand calmly
for the trimmer (and no trimmer wants to risk his life fighting
with a donkey that does not want to be trimmed). That problem can be solved by having the donkey sedated, but that too
involves additional costs.

Obesity is also a common problem. Instead of feeding the
donkey too little, some owners refuse to acknowledge that donkeys are not horses. They feed them like a horse (most commercial feeds are designed for horses) and then do not exercise
them. The donkey gradually gets fatter and fatter. Once a donkey
is obese, it is very difficult to work the excess weight off. Obesity
can lead to all kinds of health problems, including laminitis to
the hooves, which is crippling. States Dean:

Our donkeys will never be as lean as feral burros in the Southwest or working donkeys in developing countries, and we wouldn't want them to be that thin. But we have to be careful with their weight. Let's smother them with our time and attention, not food.

Most of the rescued donkeys arrive at the shelter terrified. They have either not been handled or have been handled roughly by having people pull their ears, or only putting a halter on them when they want to do something that is frightening to them. Some burros have been used for roping practice, a cruel activity that can result in broken legs, a crushed esophagus, or severe skin abrasions. As a result, the donkeys arrive very afraid of any human contact. The Longhopes staff must start all over with these donkeys in order to train them to trust humans.

Pneumonia, caused by viral or bacterial infections, is fairly common, especially in donkeys whose owners do not provide winter shelter for them. Donkeys do not have a waterproof coat like some animals. If they get cold and wet, they can catch a cold, which can quickly lead to pneumonia. Donkeys originated in North Africa and were not intended to be snow-bound. Pneumonia can be fatal to donkeys if not properly treated, but some of the donkeys at Longhopes have been able to recover from near-death pneumonia infections.

Many of Longhopes' donkeys are rescued from local sales barns where they are destined to be sold for slaughter. Since there are no longer any equine slaughter facilities in the United States, this means that the donkeys sold are shipped to slaughterhouses in Mexico to be killed and processed for foreign markets, where there is a high demand for equine meat. On the trip south in hot (or freezing), overcrowded trailers, some very young donkeys may be trampled to death and others may die from thirst.

Despite what many of the rescued animals coming to the Longhopes shelter have endured, Dean says the donkeys are remarkably intelligent, forgiving, and resilient; and most can be rehabilitated once they are in a safe, nurturing environment. On arrival at the shelter, each donkey's physical and emotional health is evaluated. Some are untamed due to owner ignorance; some are suffering physically or psychologically from mistreatment or neglect. That is why Dean and her staff often spend untold hours working with a donkey on behavioral rehabilitation. Once the animal is healthy, well-behaved, and has a set of basic skills, it has a better chance of finding and, more importantly, keeping a permanent home. Sometimes new owners travel to Longhopes for some "boot camp" training of their own, in which they learn the important basics of donkey care, such as feeding, grooming, hoof care, leading, haltering, and trailering. The staff impresses upon new owners that the adoption of a donkey is a lifetime responsibility.

To help solve the donkey overpopulation problem in the United States, no breeding is allowed at the shelter or by adopters. All jacks are castrated upon arrival. The staff at Longhopes believes that donkeys should not be bred until all existing domestic donkeys or captured wild donkeys have a good home. Adopters of jennets must agree in the adoption contract that the animal will never be used for breeding. As the Longhopes brochure points out, "We encourage recycling of donkeys instead of breeding."

Dean believes that some donkey owners are allowing too much uncontrolled breeding of too many animals, whether the purpose is for sale or the breeding was unintentional. She then added:

> *Too many donkeys are produced for the number of homes that are available. Donkeys require rescuing due to the disposable pet attitude that has plagued most other animal species. In the United States and most other industrialized countries, donkeys have lost their jobs as beasts of burden. When an equine does not provide an income, many owners become*

unwilling to spend money to get the animal necessary medical attention. The donkey is then sold for slaughter or languishes in neglect. Donkeys also present a unique problem in that they can live thirty to fifty years and thus can outlive even the most devoted owner.

With a few exceptions, Dean says it is their policy that donkeys from the shelter are adopted out only in pairs or to a home that already has a donkey. The reason is that donkeys are very social creatures and are much happier with another of their own kind. Generally a fee is charged to help defray the shelter's expenses and ensure that the adopter can afford the new pets. This fee usually does not cover the shelter's investment in the donkeys, but is generally higher than the fee charged for adopting wild donkeys from the Bureau of Land Management.

Longhopes "special guests" pose for a photograph on a chilly winter day.

Longhopes Donkey Shelter Photo

However, the donkeys rescued by Longhopes are already trained and often have received more thorough medical care than the feral donkeys. Longhopes Donkey Shelter has received and trained many of the burros that were originally purchased from Bureau of Land Management auctions.

At the time of this writing, Longhopes' fee is $175 to $400 for a single donkey (only sold if it will join another donkey or equine at its new home) and about $500 for a pair of donkeys (the pairing up often has already occurred at the shelter). If a buyer already owns a horse, the staff at Longhopes wants to make sure that a potential owner realizes the big difference between a horse and a donkey. A representative from the shelter will be glad to provide the details. Longhopes can also help bring a farm or ranch up to donkey standards. Ask about the equipment your donkey will need, and you might want to line up a trainer to work with your new animal.

When donkeys are placed, an onsite inspection is made to assure that each animal will have at least one acre of fenced pasture on the premises plus access to non-moldy grass hay, fresh, unfrozen water, and an eight-foot by sixteen-foot, three-sided loafing shed for every two animals. Regular grooming is required, especially hoof trimming. Longhopes' donkeys cannot be used for roping. Longhopes reserves the right to reclaim a donkey if the adoption "is deemed unsuccessful for any reason" during scheduled visits in the first year. Even after the adoption is finalized, Longhopes retains the right of first refusal, i.e. the donkey cannot be sold, given away, or auctioned without first giving the shelter the chance to take the animal back. In this way, Longhopes serves as a permanent safety net for their donkeys and their adopters.

Sometimes just the right person comes along at just the right time for just the right donkeys. A perfect example is the story of Etta Windwalker, who lives on a thirty-two acre ranch north of Pueblo, Colorado. She was devastated when she had to have her two donkeys (a mother and daughter) put down in July

2008, because of their worsening medical conditions. Although she owns plenty of other animals — goats, chickens, birds, dogs, cats, and even koi — she realized over time that there was a hole in her heart that only another pair of donkeys could fill. Looking on the Longhopes' adoption website, she saw a mother and daughter named "Sassy" and "Ariel," and she called Kathy Dean to inquire about them. Dean told her Sassy had been taken away from a woman who had been charged with animal abuse. When the donkey arrived at Longhopes, she was starving and had no hair. A few months later Sassy gave birth to a perfectly healthy foal. With a nutritious diet plus love and attention, Sassy, too, rebounded into good health. After Windwalker described the set-up at her ranch, Dean told her, "You have the exact home I've been envisioning for them."

Dean delivered Sassy and Ariel to Windwalker's ranch herself, bringing along two coats, two halters, and a hoof pick as

A healthy newborn foal stands next to her rescued Mom.
Lyn Bezek Photo

well as a pamphlet on hoof care and a DVD on donkey training and care. Windwalker says the two donkeys adjusted "fabulously" and now come when she honks the horn in the evenings
to get their donkey cookies and peppermint candy. "There are
wonderful people out there that open their hearts and homes
to these animals and give them a second chance," says Dean.
"That's what keeps me going."

To get just the right fit for a particular pair of donkeys, Dean
and her husband Alan are willing to deliver them to adoptive
homes as far away as Montana, Wyoming, New Mexico, and
even Tennessee. They literally go the extra mile to see that there
is a good fit between humans and donkeys, and that the new
owners will take good care of their adopted pets.

Occasionally Dean will be the go-between to expedite finding the right home for homeless donkeys that have been taken
in by another animal rescue shelter. In the winter of 2009 she
was asked to help place two young male donkeys, "Tarzan"
and "Hershey," who had ended up at an animal rescue in Cortez, Colorado. Longhopes stepped in to pay for a complicated
castration surgery (crypt orchid) for Tarzan, and then hooked
both donkeys up with the Two Mile High Club in Cripple
Creek. The two buddies are now officially part of the famous
Cripple Creek herd. Tarzan has very unusual markings on his
back and interesting stripes on all four legs, which makes it a
little easier to spot the donkey when he wanders off to play
with the horses.

Caring for the twenty to forty resident donkeys or "long-
eared guests" at any given time at the shelter takes a lot of
work and organizational skills. Dean, her husband Alan, and
three part-time employees are joined by volunteers, student
interns, and community service workers to get the job done.
Duties include feeding the donkeys twice a day, corral cleaning,
grooming, and training, as well as grant writing, transportation
of donkeys, and organizing fund-raising events. Volunteers are
always needed and welcomed.

From time to time, the donkeys at Longhopes receive grooming, socialization, and lots of enthusiastic hugs from a group of adults with developmental disabilities from the Developmental Disabilities Resource Center Recreation Department (DDRC) in Jefferson County. The calm, gentle nature of donkeys makes them natural therapists for children and anyone with special needs, and the DDRC clients always come away with new skills and new-found self-esteem. It is a win-win situation.

Sometimes a situation arises when a donkey's needs are much more complicated than they first appear. The story of "Mira" and her foal, "Bliss", illustrates the heartwrenching and complex problems that can surround a rescued donkey. In the late summer of 2000, Mira, a twelve-year-old jennet, came to Longhopes. Her owner had sold her to the slaughterhouse, and Longhopes bought her to save her. Mira was an example of extreme neglect. Her hooves were so overgrown that she could barely walk. When the farrier came to trim the donkey's hooves,

The donkeys at Longhopes Donkey Shelter have plenty of room to graze.

Pamela Moser Photo

she was unable to cut them because the hoof wall was as hard as floor tile. She suggested having Mira stand in water to soften the hooves, but Mira wanted no part of that. Shortly thereafter, Dean and staff member Sandy Usher took advantage of a fall rainstorm by kneeling beside Mira in the mud and chipping off her long hooves one-quarter inch at a time. That would be just the beginning of a long rehabilitation.

The thin frame that Mira had on arrival gradually filled out, and Dean began to suspect the donkey might be pregnant. The normal gestation period for a donkey is eleven to thirteen months. Not knowing when Mira got bred and because she was so underweight when she arrived, it was impossible to determine when Mira might foal. "We felt so bad for her because her hooves were already so painful and now she had the additional weight of a growing foal to contend with," Dean says.

On one unseasonably warm day in January, Mira was out in the pasture with the herd. Dean happened to look out her office window and noticed a commotion in the pasture. It looked to her like Mira had just had her foal and another jennet was fighting her for it. Most donkeys are very gentle and affectionate to newborn foals, so this was an unusual sight. States Dean:

> Later we learned that "Dixie," a recently received jennet, had been ripped from her foal by her former owner. The owner was anxious to get rid of Dixie, so she failed to tell us that Dixie had a foal. Sudden weaning is a cruel and lazy practice by breeders. It is also very stressful on foals (and the mothers).

When Dixie saw Mira's foal being born, she grabbed it to replace the foal she had recently lost. Mira was exhausted from giving birth and could barely walk — let alone run — to keep her foal. Dean, knowing that she had only minutes to keep the foal from being stepped on or otherwise injured in a fight, got on the phone and called for help from her neighbors. They arrived and a rescue plan was quickly devised. "We drove a pickup truck into the pasture and two people diverted Dixie from the foal long enough for me to scoop it up into the bed of the truck," she said. "If we had been able to pick up Mira, we would have done that too but she weighed over 500 pounds. Therefore, she had to follow us … back to the barn."

Mira and her foal "Bliss" were reunited in a private stall to rest. Just to be safe, a veterinarian was called in to check on mother and baby. He gave them both a clean bill of health and Bliss was clearly nursing. "We were very happy, and we saw little Bliss as a miracle given the prior neglect suffered by Mira," says Dean. "It felt like we had averted a crisis and all would be smooth sailing from then on. Unfortunately, that was not to be the case."

The weather suddenly dropped below freezing. Mira and Bliss had a thick bed of shavings and Bliss wore a sweater to help keep her warm, but it was not enough. When Bliss was three days old, Dean found Bliss at 5 a.m. almost frozen in her stall. She was not moving at all and was extremely cold. Bliss' respirations were very shallow. Dean picked her up, took her inside the house, and wrapped her in a quilt. Then Dean held Bliss on her lap in the car while Alan drove them to the nearest veterinary clinic.

The normal temperature of a donkey foal is ninety-nine to one hundred degrees. Bliss's temperature was about seventy degrees. The veterinarian gave her about a fifty-fifty chance of surviving. "We were heartbroken," says Dean, who wondered:

> *How did this happen? What did we do wrong? We were*
> *filled with guilt, but later we put the pieces together.*
> *For the first three weeks of life, a foal's only food is its*
> *mother's milk. A normal foal gains one to three pounds*
> *per day because the milk is very rich. Although Bliss*
> *was nursing, Mira was only producing about one-fifth*
> *of the milk that was necessary to sustain a growing*

Bliss is getting warm inside Kathy Dean's house.
Longhopes Donkey Shelter Photo

foal. *Poor Bliss did not have enough nutrition to (allow*
her body to) keep her warm at night, so she suffered
hypothermia.

Dean believes the likely cause of Mira's problems was Tall
Fescue Grass. In all equines, except pregnant mares and jennets, Tall Fescue Grass is a safe feed. However, in pregnant
equines it causes the mare or jennet to either abort the fetus,
produce a stillborn fetus, or fail to lactate. "We believe Mira ate
Tall Fescue Grass in the months before she arrived at Longhopes," states Dean. "Our theory was further confirmed by the
stillborn foal born the next month to another jennet that came
with Mira to Longhopes."

Dean and Alan left Bliss at the veterinary clinic, knowing
there was nothing more they could do. For the next couple of
days the veterinarian slowly warmed Bliss by keeping heated
blankets over her and tube feeding her with warm milk. It
worked. He saved Bliss.

Back at Longhopes, the little milk that Mira had been producing completely disappeared in the absence of stimulation from Bliss. Jennets who lose their foals mourn — sometimes for days. Their survival instinct, however, eventually forces them to let go and move on. The sudden removal of Bliss to the clinic forced Mira to believe her foal had died. That effectively made Bliss an orphan. It was necessary to teach Bliss to drink from a bottle. The veterinarian tried repeatedly to get Bliss to drink from a baby bottle but she would not do it. He had to put a tube down her throat to feed her. "Tubing" cannot be done by amateurs, so it was imperative that Bliss learn to drink from a bottle if Bliss was to survive.

A week passed and Bliss was still not sucking from the bottle. The veterinarian bills were mounting. In the business of rescuing animals, difficult choices have to be made every day. Money is limited and so the question has to be asked, "Can we afford to save this animal?" Dean explained:

> The time came when we had to end the veterinarian bills. Despite how much we loved Bliss, we had so many other mouths to feed and we could not jeopardize them all for one little foal. With all the obstacles Bliss faced, we wondered if maybe she was not meant to survive. So I called the vet and told him we would just have to bring Bliss home and take our chances.

The veterinarian asked to be given one more day with the foal and Dean agreed. Happily, the next day he called to tell them that Bliss had started drinking milk once he tried putting it in a beer bottle with a rubber sheep's nipple on it. Bliss was ready to come home.

Because it was still January and the temperatures were near zero, Bliss could not survive out in the barn. More importantly, since Mira no longer recognized Bliss as her foal, there was no donkey to protect Bliss and bring her in from the cold. Dean

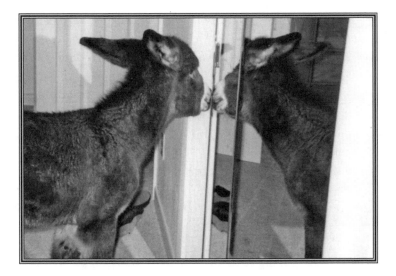

Bliss checks herself out in the mirror. A girl has to look good!
Longhopes Donkey Shelter Photo

was forced to make a little nursery for the foal in the feed room. Bliss had to be fed every two hours around the clock, so Dean and her husband took turns waking up during the night, putting on heavy winter coats and boots, and going outside to feed her. Since both Dean and her husband still worked full-time jobs away from the shelter, the 2 A.M. and 4 A.M. feedings became very difficult very quickly, and they decided they had to make a change. It was then that the "no donkeys in the house" rule was broken. They made a nursery for Bliss in their basement. "Before donkeys, my first passion was cats and eventually my husband told me I could not keep bringing stray after stray cat into the house," laughs Dean. "This led me to rescuing stray donkeys because they live in a barn and I would NEVER be trying to bring them into our home. Never say never!"

Even though they did not have to go outside anymore, waking up every two hours during the night to feed Bliss became too much to bear. Dean sent out an S.O.S. on the internet asking for any suggestions that might help with the nighttime feedings. Someone came to the rescue by suggesting they fill an insulated beverage cooler with heated milk substitute. In place of the spout they fashioned a sheep's nipple, and then wrapped the cooler with the jacket Alan had been wearing when he bottle-fed Bliss. She was drawn to it and began nursing. The cooler allowed the foal to have ten hours of warm milk available at any time, and the weary couple started sleeping through the night again.

As time went on, Bliss became lonely in her basement nursery and would be allowed to join Kathy and Alan in the living room, office, or bedroom. Housebreaking a donkey is not easy so there were accidents, but Bliss got the attention she needed. When the foal started eating solid food and grew too big to carry up and down the stairs, it was time for her to join the other donkeys in the barn. She went willingly, but by this time Bliss thought of herself as more than a donkey — she thought of herself as a human who was entitled to extra privileges. "This is a common problem with most orphan animals and is not easy to undo once the problem has been created," states Dean. "But to us, she would always be our special little wonder."

Shortly after Bliss went to the barn to join her peers, Longhopes received a telephone call from the Bureau of Land Management. Their staff had heard about Bliss and asked if the shelter would be willing to take another orphan foal. They had a jennet which had just foaled and was refusing to allow the newborn to nurse. This happens sometimes with very young jennets or with jennets that develop an infection that makes it painful when the foal tries to nurse. The Bureau of Land Management had no resources to keep an around-the clock feeding schedule. If Longhopes would not take the foal, it would have to be allowed to die.

Dean states:

> We didn't hesitate before agreeing to take the three-day-old foal, who we named "Hope." She was so tiny

when she arrived, but, unlike Bliss, Hope immediately took to bottle feeding. We were able to get her to use the beverage cooler to nurse, but there was a problem. Bliss decided she was not weaned and wanted to nurse from a bottle again because Hope was nursing. Luckily, we found a double-sided beverage cooler. With two nipples, Hope and Bliss could both nurse at the same time. This created a strong bond between the two foals and they became so inseparable that they were soon named the "Velcro Sisters."

Bliss and Hope's story has a happy ending. Two Longhopes volunteers agreed to give the foals a new home together in Castle Rock, Colorado. They also adopted two large, adult gelding donkeys to hang out with the foals and protect them until they grew up.

Mira remained at Longhopes for eight more years. Dean states:

Bliss and Hope could help themselves to milk at anytime.
Longhopes Donkey Shelter Photo

*It took years to reshape her hooves as they grew out.
When we finally thought we had her problem fixed, she
developed ringbone in her front legs and no amount
of Western or alternative treatment could reverse the
damage. Nevertheless, Mira was quiet, friendly, and
well-mannered. When the good days were few and far
between, we helped her gently pass on. Mira taught
us so much about the resilience of donkeys and their
capacity for rehabilitation. She is greatly missed.*

Today Bliss and Hope still live with their adopters in Castle Rock, along with "Bigun" (a mammoth jennet) and "Gib" (a standard gelding jack). Bliss has never lost her spirited attitude from her days as a pampered house donkey. "For this reason, we allow her to write our donkey advice column in the Longhopes newsletter," says Dean. "But she is no longer Bliss. She is now 'Miss Bliss' to her fans."

Perhaps one of the most amazing letters that Miss Bliss has ever received came from Mea Jacobs, a little girl with a very big heart. Mea's letter appeared in a 2009 Longhopes' newsletter:

*Dear Miss Bliss:
I am going to be in the second grade. I like to read, so
every story I read I get $1.00. I want your donkeys to
have my money for food and medicine. I have 4 donkeys in Illinois. They are fat! They eat lots of grass. I
want your donkeys to be fat and feel good too.*
   Love, Mea
P.S. This month I read 26 stories.

As a non-profit organization, Longhopes is supported solely through donations, adoption fees, grants, and the sale of donkey merchandise such as books and "alumni" calendars on its website: www.longhopes.org. Donations may be made for the purchase of hay (the donkeys at the shelter eat about

Mea Jacobs, seen here on one of her own donkeys, sends money that she earns from reading books to help the Longhopes donkeys.
Jacobs Family Photo

forty-six tons of hay per year) and medical supplies, or can be designated to two special funds. One is the Auction Rescue Fund that saves donkeys from the slaughterhouse. The other is the Guardianship Fund in which the donor sponsors a particular donkey in the Education and Rehabilitation Sponsorship (E.A.R.S.) Program or one in sanctuary, which means that because of advanced age or illness the animal is not adoptable and will live out its days in the peaceful environment of Longhopes. A sponsorship of a donkey that will be at the shelter for a long time, in sanctuary, or is in the E.A.R.S. program, is currently only $30 a month, but that amount could go up in the future. This sponsorship entitles the donor to special visiting rights with that donkey as well as periodic updates on "their" animals. Other specific uses for a one-time donation include such expenses as paying for surgery for a particular animal or a special diet for animals with bad or no teeth.

After ten years of working with donkeys day in and day out, Dean and her staff have acquired a wealth of knowledge and expertise about donkeys and their care. Longhopes eagerly shares that information with any donkey owner anywhere. Staff members spend hours on the phone answering medical and behavioral questions and offering advice. They also conduct training sessions at the shelter for owners and their donkeys that need to learn the ins and outs of haltering and leading, trailer loading, and preparing for the farrier. At present, volunteers Chuck Rinkor and Ross Keller even make home visits around Colorado responding to calls for help.

Training handouts and articles are given away free of charge. A training DVD covers haltering, de-spooking, gentling, grooming, hooves, leading, and trailer loading and is available at the time this book is being written to adopters for twenty dollars plus shipping and to all others for thirty-five dollars plus shipping. A donkey hoof-care training DVD was recently made by

Sometimes the burro's own winter coat is not enough in the cold Colorado winter.

Longhopes Donkey Shelter Photo

shelter staff through a grant from the Michele and Agnese Cestone Foundation and is also available for a fee. Topics include tools and safety, hoof anatomy, trimming the calm donkey, trimming the nervous donkey, hoof abnormalities, and the extreme trim. This DVD has the potential to impact donkeys across the country that are not getting adequate hoof care. Dean says they do all this outreach because "every donkey we can keep in a loving home is one less donkey that will require placement at a shelter like ours."

Not every animal that comes to Longhopes makes it out of the shelter to a new home, but while they are at the shelter they are treated with great love. Sometimes an animal's humane death must be considered. Dean tells of some of those donkeys who did not make it.

For example, "Doc" was rescued off the slaughter truck in March 2009. Dean recalls:

> *Unfortunately he had bladder stones and a tumor in his mouth. But you would never have known it — he was a darling young mammoth gelding. He was saved with his close companion "Wyatt," an eight-year-old mammoth donkey. Sadly, Doc did not survive the surgery that was needed to repair his bladder, but he did live long enough to make sure Wyatt was safe and acclimated to Longhopes. Poor Wyatt arrived with a broken ear, a nasal infection, rope scars, and open cuts on every part of his body. Surgery was required to remove the bone splinters in his nose and the scar tissue from rope burns. Luckily for Wyatt, good food, shelter, daily wound cleaning, and antibiotics healed most of his physical scars. Doc is gone but his buddy Wyatt clearly has a new lease on life.*

Dean also mentions "Rocky," who arrived in 1999 at the age of forty-three when his owner had to move.

He was a very sweet grandfather figure to the other donkeys. He had multiple generic problems, but we were determined to give him a comfortable, warm home for as long as he needed it. On a sunny day in 2001 Rocky laid down after breakfast and silently passed away. He taught us more than we can ever explain.

"Jolly" was a fifteen year old gelding donkey on his way to the slaughterhouse when he was taken in right before a big winter storm in 2005. Dean remembers:

Over the next fourteen months we tried several treatments to eliminate his chronic and congenital pain symptoms. At times we saw improvement but it was short-lived. Being unable to manage his pain and unwilling to watch him struggle to walk, Jolly was humanely euthanized in 2007. He left a good friend "Toby" and many volunteers who had become attached to him.

Dean has another story:

"Snoopy" truly was Longhopes. He arrived in 1999 and he was our mascot until he passed away in December 2008. Snoopy was about fifteen when we took him off a slaughter truck. Thin, scarred, and afraid, it took many months to earn his trust. For a long time Snoopy's health was good, and he was placed on the list of donkeys available for adoption. A few families came to meet him, but during each visit he would invariably misbehave in their presence. After several similar incidents it became clear that Snoopy had no desire to leave Longhopes, so he was made our mascot and given permanent sanctuary in the shelter. He was

the poster child for donkey rescue. He needed so much rehabilitation, and he proved what he could achieve regardless of the length of prior physical abuse and neglect. In his later years, Snoopy had his own stall (no other donkey got that treatment) for comfort and privacy. He was known as the 'Hugh Hefner' of Longhopes (without the girls). Snoopy never had any special friend at Longhopes but he did have a job. We'd make him babysit new or young donkeys!!! He hated it. Nothing will be the same without him.

In September 2009, Longhopes held an open house to celebrate their first ten years of "loving and saving donkeys." During those ten years, 440 animals were rescued (including one goat, one horse, and one mule) and over 400 were adopted out. A ten-year survey revealed that the whereabouts of ninety-one percent of the adopted donkeys was still known. Approximately ten percent of the total adoptees had returned to the shelter; but all but one percent have already found another home.

Donkeys that are getting a second chance at life at the Longhopes shelter.

Lyn Bezek Photo

"I cannot save them all," says Dean. "But I know the ones that have been saved have gotten a second chance."

A portion of the proceeds of this book will go to Longhopes Donkey Rescue Shelter. You can help save the donkeys too! Contact:

Longhopes Donkey Shelter, Inc.
Kathy Dean, Executive Director
50 South Dutch Valley Road
Bennett, Colorado 80102
Phone: (303) 644-5930
Email: adoptions@longhopes.org

CHAPTER TEN

ᗢ

Colorado's Burros
Today and Tomorrow

We know that burros have left indelible hoof prints throughout the history of the Centennial State, but what contributions are they making today and what does the future hold for them? Versatile, adaptable, and dependable, with centuries of experience in partnering with man, burros still have much to offer us and important jobs to do. Fortunately for the long-eared animals, their tasks today — as pets, tourist attractions, therapy animals, guards, hiking buddies, racers, and more — are much easier than the back-breaking work their ancestors endured as beasts of burden for prospectors, miners, and freighters.

Like dogs, burros are loyal and affectionate and make wonderful pets (jennets and geldings, that is, never jacks). Some have been known to rest their shaggy heads on their owners' shoulders or laps for long periods of time, especially while being scratched or petted. If you scratch inside or behind those long, floppy ears, you will have a friend for life. The staff at Longhopes Donkey Shelter likes to refer to the donkey as "man's other best friend." Donkey enthusiasts are as crazy about their pet donkeys as many people are about the family dog or cat.

Jon Katz, author of numerous books on border collies, writes in his essay, "Why I Own Donkeys," that his two donkeys are "the heart and soul of my farm" and have "profoundly spiritual natures." He notes that they easily attach themselves to people and even nuzzle and lean into humans that they like. As an added bonus, he remarks that "they connect me to nature and to history."

Miniature donkeys (which stand 36 inches or less at the shoulders) are becoming more and more popular as pets for children. Robert W. Green of Trenton, New Jersey was one of the first American breeders of the miniature donkey. In 1929 he imported seven of the little animals from their native island of Sardinia in the Mediterranean Sea and immediately fell in love with them. He describes the diminutive donkeys in glowing terms: "Miniature donkeys possess the affection of a Newfoundland dog, the resignation of a cow, the durability of a mule, the courage of a tiger, and the intellectual capability only slightly inferior to man's."

Burro racer John Vincent of Franktown won the 2009 Fairplay fifteen-mile short race while running with his miniature donkey "Crazy Horse." Vincent owns ten miniature donkeys and says that they make excellent pets, describing them as "especially sweet and affectionate."

George and Beth Hurd of Lake City, Colorado, acquired three miniature donkeys — "Humphrey," "Shining" ("Shiny") and "Sweet Pea" — about four years ago. As owners of the now tourist- oriented Hardtack Mine since 1994, the Hurds saw the little burros as a natural fit with their historical mining community. The three have been together since they were babies and make appearances at the Hardtack Mine to charm visitors and sometimes give the children a ride or two. They mainly

George and Beth Hurd's three miniature donkeys even have their names on their shed.

Hurd Family Photo

eat grass and hay, but are getting a bit obese from carrots and other treats sneakily provided by neighbors. In addition to their "tourist attraction" duties, the donkeys' other jobs appear to be "eating and sleeping well" (to stay healthy, of course) and serving as "very good watchdogs" in the remote, predator-prevalent environment.

At the age of eight, Humphrey is white with spots and a little bit of a cross visible on his back. Shiny, age twelve, and Sweet Pea, age ten, had the same father; but no cross is visible on Shiny's white back, while Sweet Pea's grey-dun color emphasizes the burro cross for which donkeys are known.

Beth had the same experience as author Lyn Bezek and has loved burros ever since reading *Brighty of the Grand Canyon* as a child. The little donkeys that the Hurds have now are not their first. When a county local gave the family a relatively large donkey named "Pedro" years ago, they were amazed at the affection received from their friendly and hard-working animal. Pedro became well-known in the area, as he wandered up and down Henson Creek from their house to the mine. The donkey "disgracefully" ate the treats that seasonal campers along the creek gave him. The Hurd family gave Pedro to the local UPS lady, who then used him to help train her colts.

Four miniature donkeys manage to steal the hearts of children and adults alike at the Country Boy Mine in Breckenridge, where they live year-round. The mine, which was first worked in 1887 and closed in 1948, is now open twelve months a year as a tourist attraction to show visitors what mining was like back in its heyday. The Country Boy Mine produced gold and silver in its early operation and later on mainly lead and zinc for use in both World Wars. According to mine tour guide Austin Kriete, the job of the resident miniature donkeys is to add ambiance to the mine tour experience. They stay in a warm barn at night but roam freely during the day, receiving lots of grain treats that the

Visitors crowd around the miniature donkeys at the Hard Tack Mine near Lake City.

Hurd Family Photo

visitors buy for them from an old-fashioned gumball machine that is kept on the grounds. "They are loving and gentle and love to be petted," states Kriete. "These four have it a lot easier than their predecessors did, that's for sure."

Two burros captured by the Bureau of Land Management in Arizona's Sonoran Desert have secure jobs as the official mascots of the Western Museum of Mining and Industry north of Colorado Springs. Since July 2001, "Oro" and "Nugget" have been greeting visitors, including hundreds of school groups, who come to the museum to learn about Colorado's mining heritage. Local Sertoma Club members and Girl Scout Troop 516 helped with the initial corral maintenance in the burros' five-acre pasture. On an ongoing basis several Boy Scout troops in the vicinity donate money from aluminum recycling projects to pay for hay and oat treats for Oro and Nugget. Two special burro-related events are held each year. In March the museum sponsors "Spring Break with the Burros," a one-day event when children and their families can feed carrots to the two mascots and learn about the important part their burro ancestors played during the mining era. In August Oro and Nugget are the guests of honor at the "Burro Birthday Bluegrass Bash," which features a day of toe-tapping music and a giant birthday cake.

Because of their calm, patient nature, burros and donkeys of any size are often used to teach children and handicapped people to ride, perhaps before they graduate to larger, more high-strung horses. However, riders often prefer to stay with the burro. Its small size, affectionate nature, and slow and deliberate pace make the burro perfect for this purpose, and a very unique and special bond usually develops. Burro racer Hal Walter, who owns one jack and three geldings, notices that when his young son is on the back of one of the burros, the animal seems to sense it has precious cargo on board and steps extra carefully along the trail.

Donkeys are also still used for their calming effect on horses with which they are pastured. If a donkey is pastured with a mare and her foal, the foal might even turn to the donkey for support after it has been weaned from its mother. The donkey has a calming, steadying influence on a foal and reduces the trauma it may experience when weaned. Since most donkeys will readily approach a human, the foal often follows along and this type of behavior is quickly learned and instills a friendly attitude towards people.

Burros and miniature donkeys are also often used as stable companions. Nervous horses usually seem to calm down when donkeys or burros are around. For this reason, donkeys are often placed with racehorses, quarter horses, and show horses. They also work well with an injured horse. Miniature donkeys are usually used if they will be in the same stall as the horse, as they do not take up as much room.

As previously mentioned, a standard donkey can be very useful when halter-breaking young foals or calves. The way it works is the donkey's collar is connected to the rope attached to the

A miniature donkey tries to sneak a snack at the Country Boy Mine in Breckenridge.

Lyn Bezek Photo

halter of the animal that is being trained to lead. The donkey goes wherever it wants, basically pulling the calf or foal along with it. This way the human trainer is not associated with the bad times, but the young animals are still learning to follow a lead.

Whether in official or unofficial roles, donkeys make good therapists. Like all animals, but unlike humans, donkeys are experts at living in the present, not wasting time dwelling on the past or worrying about the future. Hanging out with donkeys helps people stay in the moment, too. Those oversized ears, fuzzy noses, soulful eyes, comical brays, and peaceful personalities all add up to a natural antidepressant that can pull a person out of the doldrums when he or she is feeling down.

Donkeys are good listeners, they never judge you, and they really do not care if you are having a bad hair day (because they're probably having one too). So the next time you are feeling depressed, do not grab a pill or a drink. Go grab a donkey and give him a gentle big hug — there are no side-effects and you will not wake up with a hangover in the morning.

One famous little foal named "Primrose" became an official therapy donkey after having one of its hind legs amputated following an attack by neighborhood dogs in 1998. Owned by Bill Lee, Primrose was successfully fitted with an artificial leg at Colorado State University's Veterinary Teaching Hospital in Fort Collins. It was the first time a prosthesis was tried on a donkey. Primrose went on to produce a foal and also to become a friend of and "spokes-animal" for children who have had amputations. "Realistically, I should have probably put the baby (Primrose) down," Lee states. "But I felt responsible. I buy and raise these animals, and I feel I have to take care of them."

Lee, a burro racer and alias "Red Tail the Mountain Man," has more than thirty burros among the 100 animals at his Laughing Valley Ranch, which includes a petting zoo. For the past eighteen summers, he has taken a few of his animals on weekend trips to Keystone Resort to set up a mini petting zoo as well as offer burro rides. As opposed to some horses, the

Sassy excels as a guard for goats near Avondale, Colorado.
Lyn Bezek Photo

burros are always calm, tender, and trustworthy. "The donkeys are always very gentle and patient with the children," he states. "They seem to know that they are (dealing with) babies."

Another job that many Colorado burros now have and excel at is that of guarding cattle, sheep, goats, and even free-ranging chickens. With their keen vision and hearing, guard donkeys can easily detect intruders such as coyotes, foxes, or unfriendly dogs, and then dispatch them with a well-placed kick or a mighty shaking of their powerful jaws. Their braying can also alert the owner and sometimes is enough by itself to scare off the predators.

Most experts on donkey behavior agree that jennets are the best choice for guard duties, noting that intact jacks have been known to injure or even kill the very livestock that they are guarding. Also a single sentry is the best because having too many guard donkeys may mean that they bond with each other instead of their charges. The ideal tactic is to acquire a jennet at a young age so that she will bond with the animals she guards.

That is exactly the course taken by Shelly Riddock of Avondale, Colorado. She adopted her jennet Sassy in 2000, when she was four months of age. Sassy's mother was part of a herd of donkeys that guarded a whole flock of sheep for a local veterinarian. Riddock states that Sassy grew up to be an amazingly effective guard for her goats. "When she detects a coyote or a strange dog, she will kick the fence first to give a warning. If the intruder keeps coming, Sassy will grab the animal by the nape of the neck with her teeth and shake it hard enough to break its neck." Riddock says her donkey's ears are the true barometer of what is going on at the farm. "My dogs can be barking and I don't pay too much attention," she states. "But if Sassy's ears go up, I know something is about to happen."

Two advantages that a donkey has over a guard dog are that it stays with the herd, no matter how far away from camp the sheep or goats roam, and the donkey does not have to be fed a diet that is any different than the animals that it is guarding. The donkey will also bed down with the other animals at night. Miniature and Mammoth Donkeys are usually not used for guard animals, as the former is usually too small and the latter is usually too slow. However, burro racer Dave TenEyck, whose miniature racing burro "Matchless" now has a second career as a guard donkey for sheep, thinks jennets often make the best protectors because of their natural maternal instincts. He says, "Nothing wants to mess with an angry mother burro or with her natural or 'adopted' children."

Burros also make good hiking buddies on the trail or in the Colorado backcountry. They can carry your pack, help keep you safe from predators, be a good companion, and even carry you home if there is an accident. Some of the donkeys at Bill Lee's Laughing Valley Ranch are trained for packing and used all over Colorado. His website states: "Our expert assistance will show how to properly pack a donkey, balancing the weight it will carry, and how to maneuver and motivate the animal up steep mountain trails, across creeks, and along roadways." For senior citizens who no longer are willing or able to carry a heavy backpack yet are not ready to give up enjoying wilderness treks, a pack burro can carry the load — and at a leisurely pace that allows everyone to slow down and smell the columbines.

As already detailed in Chapter Eight, some Colorado burros are enlisted for burro racing, but they are much more than just a racing animal. To keep them in top condition, they are fed a healthy diet, are given plenty of exercise, and receive lots of attention. The human racers usually forge very tight bonds with their burro counterparts. Burro racer Ralph Herzog says simply: "They become part of the family." And racer Curtis Imrie states: "My donkeys are my partners, my family. As I get older, they even act as my walker to get me up the pass."

Sometimes donkeys are called upon for seasonal work, such as participating in living Nativity scenes at Christmas or religious pageants on Palm Sunday and Good Friday. In Vail, Colorado, two donkeys chosen for roles in the Eagle River Presbyterian Church's living Nativity escaped from their fenced-in pen the morning before their scheduled performance. A church member and a sheriff's deputy were able to track them to the railroad tracks by following their hoofprints in the snow. The two escapees were taken back to the church just in time for the show to go on.

In Pueblo, Colorado, a Christmas Posada, which includes a donkey, has taken place every holiday season for the past thirty years. The musical procession features a young woman dressed as Mary astride a donkey and accompanied by a young man portraying Joseph as they re-enact their long journey in search of shelter. School groups and choirs perform at stops along the way and then join the procession as it continues along Main Street to its destination at the courthouse, where a living Nativity scene is performed. A calm, docile donkey that is not bothered by singing and crowds is required for this particular role, and many have answered the call over the years.

A once-in-a-lifetime role was bestowed upon Curtis Imrie's burro "Mordecai" at the January, 2008, National Western Stock Show, when he was selected to be the party mascot at the upcoming Democratic National Convention in Denver that summer. Mordecai's decision to roll around on his back in the arena clinched the vote in his favor. The burro was just scratching an itch as most burros will do; but, in this case, timing was everything. Mordecai and Imrie made several public appearances during the course of the convention. The humble, stalwart donkey has been the symbol of the Democratic Party since the days of Andrew Jackson.

Of course donkeys are still used to produce mules, prospect, haul freight, and pull small carts; and they have also shown up in some marketing campaigns such as the little donkey that wants to become a Budweiser Clydesdale and the donkeys that are shown with the World Famous Vienna Lipizzaner Stallions. Donkeys are sometimes used for comic relief in donkey polo, donkey basketball, rodeos, and with clowns; but for the most part this abusive treatment seems to be subsiding.

Having an easier life is long overdue and much deserved by the burro after all the hardships and abuse it has endured

Oro and Nugget are always a great hit at the Western Museum of Mining and Industry near Colorado Springs.

Lyn Bezek Photo

through the centuries. In fact, the burro has not only been underappreciated and ignored but has frequently been the butt of jokes. Is that because of its long ears? Its funny-sounding voice? Its scientific name of *Equus asinus*? Why did the burro get the bad reputation of being stubborn, stupid, and lazy, when in reality it is cautious, smart, and hard-working? Curtis Imrie likes to highlight this quote from Mark Twain:

> There is no character, howsoever good and fine, but it can be destroyed by ridicule, howsoever poor and witless. Observe the ass for instance: his character is about perfect. He is the choicest spirit among all humble animals, yet see what ridicule has brought him to. Instead of feeling complimented when we are called an ass, we are left in doubt.

According to Frank Brookshier in his book, *The Burro*, those who were closest to the burro down through the years knew its true worth and did not want it to be forgotten. Brookshire writes:

> While the prospector, the miner, the sheepherder, the wood hauler, the trapper, the freighter may not have had the means or influence to honor the loyal little burro, they did what they could to see that he was remembered: they named places for him. In Montezuma County, high in the Colorado Rockies, is Burro Peak. There is Burro Mountain in Rio Blanco and Burro Canyon in Las Animas. In Ouray County runs Burro Creek.... Thus, though there are few formal monuments to the burro, humble men have seen to it that places where his hooves have trod are stamped with his name, evoking an era when his long ears and his loud bray signaled that he was present and accounted for.

Another writer, Raymond Carlson, who was editor of *Arizona Highways* for many years, wrote in the December, 1940 issue of the magazine about a tough, battered burro named "Old Bill."

> *He's no beauty and he's about as awkward as a weather-beaten barn but he's as reliable as the sun itself and you can rely on him like on your best friend…. Nope! Old Bill will never win any beauty contest and those flop ears of his will seldom set an artist crazy. But sometime, maybe, they'll build a big statue out of solid granite that will stand always in honor and memory of one of the most important figures in the winning of our West and they'll dedicate it to the burro — one like Old Bill.*

In fact, the burro has been honored in Colorado with several monuments and statues. Besides the famous Prunes Monument and the World Championship Winners Monument in Fairplay, life-size bronze sculptures of burros are found in front of the middle school and high school in Fairplay, as well as in Breckenridge, Cripple Creek, and at the Colorado School of Mines in Golden.

The very best way to honor the present-day burro is to treat it with the love and respect it deserves. Fortunately, many Colorado burros have a lot of good people with big hearts on their side. The beloved Cripple Creek donkeys have the Two Mile High Club and a whole town watching out for them. Kathy Dean and her staff at Longhopes Donkey Shelter in Bennett not only rescue and rehabilitate homeless donkeys but make it their mission in life to share their donkey expertise with the world. Veteran burro racers Curtis Imrie, Hal Walter, Dave TenEyck, Ralph Herzog, John Vincent, Bill Lee, and Barb Dolan relish sharing their passion for burro racing and their love of long ears with any uninitiated newcomers; and donkey owners like Shelley Riddock and Etta Windwalker make sure their adopted donkeys

Bronze sculpture in front of the Fairplay middle and high schools honors burros.

Lyn Bezek Photo

have everything they need—from regular hoof-trimming and dental care to donkey cookies and peppermint candy.

Says Riddock: "I feel if I can take really good care of my one donkey that somehow that helps make up a little bit for the donkeys that are abused and neglected." Several years ago she designed her own Christmas card that featured her donkey Sassy and the manger scene on the front and inside contained this verse written by an anonymous author:

> *It could have been me.....*
> *I could have been the donkey*
> *on that special night*
> *that carried Mary to lay the*
> *baby Jesus in a bed of straw.*

It could have been me…
the donkey who was proud and
strong to trudge miles over
rough terrain with only
a star to guide me.

I could have been the donkey
and maybe I was
so the next time that we meet
Look into my eyes and wonder
If it could have been me.

What does the future hold for the donkeys of Colorado? If one donkey enthusiast's pronouncement is true —"to know a donkey is to love a donkey"— then more exposure to donkeys

Christmas card of Shelly Riddock honoring Sassy and her breed.

and education about them are the obvious keys to better understanding and treatment of them. If efforts to make burro racing the state's official sport are successful, increased exposure and publicity will almost certainly follow. If people like Bill Lee as Red Tail the Mountain Man continue to teach children about burros through storytelling (a Bureau of Land Management burro named "Bambi" accompanies him to carry his props and supplies) and by having kids feed and groom some of his burros at summer camps, then some of the negative myths about donkeys will begin to fade.

Donkeys themselves have much to teach us, if we choose to listen. Animal rights activist Cleveland Amory believed all animals had much to teach us. He wrote: "Only when we learn to live and let live with our fellow creatures will we finally learn to live and let live with each other." Curtis Imrie echoes those sentiments: "When we start treating donkeys right, then we'll finally have social and economic justice."

This is the way a donkey should be treated! Children feed miniature donkeys at the Country Boy Mine.

Lyn Bezek Photo

So if you get a chance to adopt a donkey or backpack with a donkey or race with a donkey or just hang out for a while with a donkey, take it. One thing is pretty much guaranteed to happen — that donkey will leave hoofprints all over your heart.

Appendix A

ಬಂ

Bold face type indicates revisions to the Wild Free Roaming Horse and Burro Act (Public Law 92-195). Sections 2. and 3. were modified by the Public Rangelands Improvement Act of 1978; Section 9. was modified by the Federal Land Policy and Management Act of 1976.

THE WILD FREE-ROAMING HORSES AND BURROS ACT OF 1971 (PUBLIC LAW 92-195)

To require the protection, management, and control of wild free- roaming horses and burros on public lands. Be it enacted by the Senate and House of Representatives of the United States of America in Congress assembled, *That Congress finds and declares that wild free-roaming horses and burros are living symbols of the historic and pioneer spirit of the West; that they contribute to the diversity of life forms within the Nation and enrich the lives of the American people; and that these horses and burros are fast disappearing from the American scene.* It is the policy of Congress that wild free-roaming horses and burros shall be protected from capture, branding, harassment, or death; and to accomplish this they are to be considered in the area where presently found, as an integral part of the natural system of the public lands.

Sec. 2. As used in this Act-

a. "Secretary" means the Secretary of the Interior when used in connection with public lands administered by him through the Bureau of Land Management and the Secretary of Agriculture in connection with public lands administered by him through the Forest Service;

b. "wild free-roaming horses and burros" means all unbranded and unclaimed horses and burros on public lands of the United States;

c. "range" means the amount of land necessary to sustain an existing herd or herds of wild free-roaming horses and burros, which does not exceed their known territorial limits, and which is devoted principally but not necessarily exclusively to their welfare in keeping with the multiple-use management concept for the public lands;

    d. "herd" means one or more stallions and his mares; and

    e. "public lands" means any lands administered by the Secretary of the Interior through the Bureau of Land Management or by the Secretary of Agriculture through the Forest Service.

    f. "excess animals" means wild free-roaming horses or burros (1) which have been removed from an area by the Secretary pursuant to application law or, (2) which must be removed from an area in order to preserve and maintain a thriving natural ecological balance and multiple-use relationship in that area.

Sec. 3.

    a. All wild free-roaming horses and burros are hereby declared to be under the jurisdiction of the Secretary for the purpose of management and protection in accordance with the provisions of this Act. The Secretary is authorized and directed to protect and manage wild free-roaming horses and burros as components of the public lands, and he may designate and maintain specific ranges on public lands as sanctuaries for their protection and preservation, where the Secretary after consultation with the wildlife agency of the State wherein any such range is proposed and with the Advisory Board established in section 7 of this Act deems such action desirable. The Secretary shall manage wild free-roaming horses and burros in a manner that is designed to achieve and maintain a thriving natural ecological balance on the public lands. He shall consider the recommendations of qualified scientists in the field of biology and ecology, some of whom shall be independent of both Federal and State agencies and may include members of the Advisory Board established in section 7 of this Act. All management activities shall be at the minimal feasible level and shall be carried out in consultation with the wildlife agency of the State wherein such lands are located in order to protect the natural ecological balance of all wildlife species which inhabit such lands, particularly endangered wildlife species. Any adjustments in forage allocations on any such lands shall take into consideration the needs of other wildlife species which inhabit such lands.

    b.

    1. The Secretary shall maintain a current inventory of wild free-roaming horses and burros on given areas of the public lands. The purpose of such inventory shall be to: make determinations as to whether and where an overpopulation exists and whether action should be taken to remove excess animals; determine appropriate management levels of wild free-roaming horses and burros on these areas of the public lands; and determine whether appro-

priate management levels should be achieved by the removal or destruction of excess animals, or other options (such as sterilization, or natural controls on population levels). In making such determinations the Secretary shall consult with the United States Fish and Wildlife Service, wildlife agencies of the State or States wherein wild free-roaming horses and burros are located, such individuals independent of Federal and State government as have been recommended by the National Academy of Sciences, and such other individuals whom he determines have scientific expertise and special knowledge of wild horse and burro protection, wild-life management and animal husbandry as related to rangeland management.

2. Where the Secretary determines on the basis of (i) the current inventory of lands within his jurisdiction; (ii) information contained in any land use planning completed pursuant to section 202 of the Federal Land Policy and Management Act of 1976; (iii) information contained in court ordered environmental impact statements as defined in section 2 of the Public Rangelands Improvement Act of 1978; and (iv) such additional information as becomes available to him from time to time, including that information developed in the research study mandated by this section, or in the absence of the information contained in (i-iv) above on the basis of all information currently available to him, that an overpopulation exists on a given area of the public lands and that action is necessary to remove excess animals, he shall immediately remove excess animals from the range so as to achieve appropriate management levels. Such action shall be taken, in the following order and priority, until all excess animals have been removed so as to restore a thriving natural ecological balance to the range, and protect the range from the deterioration associated with overpopulation:

a. The Secretary shall order old, sick, or lame animals to be destroyed in the most humane manner possible;

b. The Secretary shall cause such number of additional excess wild free-roaming horses and burros to be humanely captured and removed for private maintenance and care for which he determines an adoption demand exists by qualified individuals, and for which he determines he can assure humane treatment and care (including proper transportation, feeding, and handling): Provided, That, not more than four animals may be adopted per year by any individual unless the Secretary determines in writing that such individual is capable of humanely caring for more than four animals, including the transportation of such animals by the adopting party; and [PRIA 10/25/1978]

c. The Secretary shall cause additional excess wild free roaming horses and burros for which an adoption demand by qualified individuals does not exist to be destroyed in the most humane and cost efficient manner possible.

3. For the purpose of furthering knowledge of wild horse and burro population dynamics and their interrelationship with wildlife, forage and water resources, and assisting him in making his determination as to what constitutes excess animals, the Secretary shall contract for a research study of such animals with such individuals independent of Federal and State government as may be recommended by the National Academy of Sciences for having scientific expertise and special knowledge of wild horse and burro protection, wildlife management and animal husbandry as related to rangeland management. The terms and outline of such research study shall be determined by a redesign panel to be appointed by the President of the National Academy of Sciences. Such study shall be completed and submitted by the Secretary to the Senate and House of Representatives on or before January 1, 1983.

c. Where excess animals have been transferred to a qualified individual for adoption and private maintenance pursuant to this Act and the Secretary determines that such individual has provided humane conditions, treatment and care for such animal or animals for a period of one year, the Secretary is authorized upon application by the transferee to grant title to not more than four animals to the transferee at the end of the one-year period.

d. Wild free-roaming horses and burros or their remains shall lose their status as wild free-roaming horses or burros and shall no longer be considered as falling within the purview of this Act- (1) upon passage of title pursuant to subsection (c) except for the limitation of subsection (c)(1) of this section, or (2) if they have been transferred for private maintenance or adoption pursuant to this Act and die of natural causes before passage of title; or (3) upon destruction by the Secretary or his designee pursuant to subsection (b) of this section; or (4) if they die of natural causes on the public lands or on private lands where maintained thereon pursuant to section 4 and disposal is authorized by the Secretary or his designee; or (5) upon destruction or death for purposes of or incident to the program authorized in section 3 of this Act; Provided, That no wild free-roaming horse or burro or its remains may be sold or transferred for consideration for processing into commercial products.

Sec. 4. If wild free-roaming horses or burros stray from public lands onto privately owned land, the owners of such land may inform the nearest Federal marshall or agent of the Secretary, who shall arrange to have the animals removed. In no event shall such wild free-roaming horses and burros be destroyed except by the agents of the Secretary. Nothing in this section shall be construed to prohibit a private landowner from maintaining wild free-roaming horses or burros on his private lands, or lands leased from the Government, if he does so in a manner that protects them from harassment, and if the animals were not willfully removed or enticed from the public lands. Any individuals who maintain such wild free-roaming horses and burros on their private lands or lands leased from the Government shall notify the appropriate agent of the Secretary and supply him with a reasonable approximation of the number of animals so maintained.

Sec. 5. A person claiming ownership of a horse or burro on the public lands shall be entitled to recover it only if recovery is permissible under the branding and estray laws of the State in which the animal is found.

Sec. 6. The Secretary is authorized to enter into cooperative agreements with other landowners and with the State and local governmental agencies and may issue such regulations as he deems necessary for the furtherance of the purposes of this Act.

Sec. 7. The Secretary of the Interior and the Secretary of Agriculture are authorized and directed to appoint a joint advisory board of not more than nine members to advise them on any matter relating to wild free-roaming horses and burros and their management and protection. They shall select as advisers persons who are not employees of the Federal or State Governments and whom they deem to have special knowledge about protection of horses and burros, management of wildlife, animal husbandry, or natural resources management. Members of this board shall not receive reimbursement except for travel and other expenditures necessary in connection with their services.

Sec. 8.

a. Any person who-

1. willfully removes or attempts to remove a wild free- roaming horse or burro from the public lands, without authority from the Secretary, or

2. converts a wild free-roaming horse or burro to private use, without authority from the Secretary, or

3. maliciously causes the death or harassment of any wild free-roaming horse or burro, or

4. processes or permits to be processed into commercial products the remains of a wild free-roaming horse or burro, or

5. sells, directly or indirectly, a wild free-roaming horse or burro maintained on private or leased land pursuant to section 4 of this Act, or the remains thereof, or

6. willfully violates a regulation issued pursuant to this Act, shall be subject to a fine of not more than $2,000, or imprisonment for not more than one year, or both. Any person so charged with such violation by the Secretary may be tried and sentenced by any United States commissioner or magistrate designated for that purpose by the court by which he was appointed, in the same manner and subject to the same conditions as provided for in section 3401, title 18, United States Code.

b. Any employee designated by the Secretary of the Interior or the Secretary of Agriculture shall have power, without warrant, to arrest any person committing in the presence of such employee a violation of this Act or any regulation made pursuant thereto, and to take such person immediately for examination or trail before an officer or court of competent jurisdiction, and shall have power to execute any warrant or other process issued by an officer or court of competent jurisdiction to enforce the provisions of this Act or regulations made pursuant thereto. Any judge of a court established under the laws of the United States, or any United States magistrate may, within his respective jurisdiction, upon proper oath or affirmation showing probable cause, issue warrants in all such cases.

Sec. 9. In administering this Act, the Secretary may use or contract for the use of helicopters or, for the purpose of transporting captured animals, motor vehicles. Such use shall be undertaken only after a public hearing and under the direct supervision of the Secretary or of a duly authorized official or employee of the Department. The provisions of subsection (a) of the Act of September 8, 1959 (73 Stat. 470; 18 U.S.C. 47(a)) shall not be applicable to such use. Such use shall be in accordance with humane procedures prescribed by the Secretary.

Sec. 10. Nothing in this Act shall be construed to authorize the Secretary to relocate wild free-roaming horses or burros to areas of the public lands where they do not presently exist.

Sec. 11. After the expiration of thirty calendar months following the date of enactment of this Act, and every twenty-four calendar months thereafter, the Secretaries of the Interior and Agriculture will submit to Congress a joint report on the administration of this Act, including a summary of enforcement and/or other actions taken thereunder, costs, and such recommendations for legislative or other actions he might deem appropriate.

The Secretary of the Interior and the Secretary of Agriculture shall consult with respect to the implementation and enforcement of this Act and to the maximum feasible extent coordinate the activities of their respective departments and in the implementation and enforcement of this Act. The Secretaries are authorized and directed to undertake those studies of the habits of wild free-roaming horses and burros that they may deem necessary in order to carry out the provisions of this Act.

Appendix B

ℒℴℂ

RULES... IN PACK BURRO RACING ???

Entry Fees:
Each entrant or his sponsor will pay a fee determined by the town race director. All funds will be used for part of the prize money. This fee must accompany the entry application and will not be refunded.

Liability:
No city, private-property owners along the course, sponsoring businesses, governmental agencies, persons or organizations will be responsible in case of accident or injury to contestants. Each entrant must sign a waiver and/or release of responsibility.

Burro:
The following is the definition of a burro and is to be used in selecting a burro. The word burro comes from the Spanish word meaning donkey. A donkey is defined as being an ass. They have chestnuts on the forelegs only, while other animals of the same species, such as mules or horses, have them on hind and forelegs. The tail has no hair, except on its lower part, which has a brush. A registered veterinarian shall have the authority to disqualify any contestant and animal that does not match the above description, or whose animal is sick, doped, injured, or mistreated. The veterinarian will check the animal before and after the race. Winning burros can be held in a designated area by the race committee for 30 minutes for checking by the veterinarian. All runners must keep their burros under control. This is especially true for runners with jacks. Any burro (jacks particularly) that interferes with another runner or burro may be disqualified.

Equipment:
Each burro will be required to be equipped with a regulation pack saddle packed with prospector's paraphernalia and must include a pick, shovel, and gold pan. There shall be no minimum weight requirement for burros measuring 40 inches or less at the shoulder. For all others the combined weight of the pack saddle and paraphernalia shall be a minimum of 33 pounds.

It is strongly recommended that all participants carry at least one quart of water, food (an energy bar), and clothing (such as a windbreaker). Water, food and clothing worn during the race shall not be part of the 33 pounds. This weight will be checked at the start and finish of the race. Loss of all or part of the pack and paraphernalia will eliminate the contestant.

The burro will be led by a halter to which is attached a rope not to exceed 15 feet in length. This rope may be single knotted or looped. It is recommended that the rope be one inch-diameter or larger. No other rope or strap may be attached to either the burro or the saddle. A regulation halter must be used.

Jack chains may be used only if used with a pressure-release technique. (A jack chain is a chain or strap which is used to apply pressure over the muzzle, under the chin, or through the mouth.) Any racer coming across the finish line with nose and/or chin injuries on the animal resulting from the jack chain will be disqualified.

Cruelty:

Any contestant mistreating his animal may be disqualified. No needles, electric prods, narcotics, clubs or whips, other than the halter rope, may be used.

Course:

The race route must be followed. It will be marked by signs, people, or aid stations. Do not cut across switchbacks. Any burro leaving the course must be returned to the course without shortening the distance of the course. Any runner becoming separated from their burro (i.e., burro and runner are no longer racing as a connected team or unit) must return to the place they became separated before continuing the race. Failure to follow these rules will result in disqualification.

Team:

Contestant and burro starting the race must remain a team throughout the contest. No assistants will be allowed to accompany any team.

Winning Team:

The winning combination consists of man, or woman, and burro which must cross the finish line as a unit. The man or woman may be leading or following the burro but the burro's nose crossing the finish line first constitutes the winner.

No Riding:

The runner may push, pull, drag or carry the burro. The contestant shall at no time progress except under his own power.

Appeals:

Should a contestant be disqualified by a race official, he may continue the race (a second offense will definitely put him off the trail) and he may appeal his grievance to the race director. The decisions of the race director will be final.

Ties:

In the event of a tie, the prize money involved, if any, will equally divided by the contestants involved.

Firearms:

Carrying and use of firearms will not be permitted.

Bibliography

Books and Articles

Athearn, Frederic, *A Forgotten Kingdom, The Spanish Frontier in Colorado and New Mexico, 1540-1821*, Bureau of Land Management, Denver, 1989

Bacus, Harriet Fish, *Tomboy Bride*, Self-Published, Boulder, 1969.

Bancroft, Caroline, *Two Burros of Fairplay*, Johnson Publishing Company, Boulder, 1967

Bjorklund, Linda, *Burros!*, self-published, 2006.

Bueler, William M., *Roof of the Rockies*, Pruett Publishing Co., Boulder, 1974

Brookshier, *The Burro*, University of Oklahoma Press, 1974

Carey, Alex M., *Memories, Scenes, and Humorous Highlights of Lake City*, Self-published, Lake City, 1961.

Cornelius, Temple H., *Sheepherder's Gold*, Sage Books, Denver, 1964

Davidson, Levette J., "Rocky Mountain Burro Tales", *Denver Brand Book*, Vol. VI, Denver, 1950

Darley, Rev. George, *Pioneering in the San Juans*, Western Reflections Publishing, reprint 2008

Dyer, Rev. John L., *The Snowshoe Itinerant*, Western Reflections Publishing, reprint 2008

Ellis, Anne, *The Life of an Ordinary Woman*, First Mariner Books Edition, New York, 1999

Friggens, Myriam, *Tales, Trails and Tommyknockers*, Johnson Publishing, Boulder, 1979

Gibbons, Rev. J. J., *In the San Juans*, Western Reflections Publishing

Grey, Zane, *Tappan's Burro*, Harper Collins Publishing, New York, 1923

Griffiths, Mel, *San Juan Country*, Pruett Press, Boulder, Colorado, 1984

Henn, Roger, *Lies, Legends, and Lore of the San Juans*, Western Reflections Publishing Co., Ouray, Co, 1999

Henry, Marguerite, *Brighty of the Grand Canyon*, Rand McNally and Company, 1953

Ingham, G. Thomas, *Digging Gold Among the Rockies*, Edgewood Publishing Co., 1882, Reprinted by Western Reflections Publishing, 2009,

Jack, Ellen E., *The Fate of a Fairy*, M. A. Donehue & Co., Chicago, 1910, Reprinted by Western Reflections Publishing, 2010

Kindquist, Cathy, *Stony Pass*, San Juan Book Company, Silverton, Colorado, 1987

Lakes, Arthur, *Prospecting for Gold and Silver*, 1895, Reprinted by Western Reflections Publishing, 2010

Lewis, J. H., "Rocky Mountain Burros", *Our Country West,* The Companion Series, Perry Mason and Company, Boston, 1897

Moynihan, Ruth B., Armitage, Susan, and Dischamp, Christine Fisher, *So Much to Be Done,* University of Nebraska Press, Lincoln, Nebraska, 1990

McCandless, H. M., *The Burro Book*, Self Published, Pueblo, Co, 1900

Noel, Thomas J., *The Colorado Almanac: Facts About Colorado,* Graphics Arts center, Portland

Raine, William M. and Barnes, Will C., *Cattle*, Doran and Co., Garden City, N.Y., 1930

Reyher, Ken, *Antoine Rubidoux and Fort Uncompahgre*, Western reflections Publishing Co., Ouray Colorado, 1998

Reyher, Ken, *Silver and Sawdust,* Western Reflections Publishing Co., Ouray, CO, 2000

Rickard, T. A., *Journeys of Observation*, Dewey Publishing Co., San Francisco, 1907

Roberts, Dan, *A Story of the Centennial State,* Eagle Tail Press, Grand Junction, CO, 1973

Simmons, Virginia M., *The San Luis Valley*, Second Edition, University of Colorado Press, Boulder, 1999

Smith, P. David, *Exploring the Historic San Juan Triangle*, Wayfinder Press, Ridgway, CO, 2004

Smith, P. David, *Mountains of Silver*, Western Reflections Publishing Co., Ouray, CO, 1994

Smith, P. David, *The Road That Silver Built, The Million Dollar Highway*, Western Reflections Publishing Co., Lake City, CO, 2009

Sprague, Marshall, *Money Mountain*, Little, Brown and Co., Boston, 1953

Tobias, Michael and Morrison, Jane, *Donkeys: The Mystique of Equus Asinus*, San Francisco, 2006

Trenary, Melissa, *Donkeys of the Gold Camp—An Informational Guide to Cripple Creek's World Famous Donkey Herd*, Jackass Productions, Cripple Creek, 2009

Vanderbusche, Duane, *Early Days in the Gunnison Country*, Self-Published, Gunnison, CO, 1976

Walter, Hal, *Pack Burro Stories*, Out There! Publishing, 1998

Waters, Frank, *Midas of the Rockies*, Sage Books, Denver, 1937

William's Tourist Guide and Map of the San Juan Mines of Colorado, 1876

Young, Jr., Otis, *Western Mining*, University of Oklahoma Press, Norman, OK, 1970

Websites

www.blackbeautyranch.com

www.countryboymine.com

www.donkeys.com

www.donkey derby days.com

www.en.wikipedia.org, burros

www.fundforanimals.com

www.laughingvalleyranch.com

www.longhopes.org

www.lovelongears.com

www.packburroracing.com

www.wildhorseandburro.blm.gov

www.wmmi.org (Western Museum of Mining and Industry)

Newspapers and Magazines

Abbey, Robert V., "Many Myths in Wild Horse Management," *Salt Lake Tribune,* January 10, 2010

"A Friendly Tale: Burros Airlifted from the Depths of the Grand Canyon Become Ranch Residents," The Fund for Animals Website, September 26, 2006

Allen, Lynn, "America's Beasts of Burden," *Colorado Country Life Magazine*, August 2008

American Magazine, December 1949

Boulder Weekly, August 2, 1907, "Leaders of the Pack" by David Phillips

Carlson, Raymond, "Old Bill, Portrait of an Arizonan," *Arizona Highways*, December, 1940

Cowen, John L., "Apotheosis of the Ass," *Overland Magazine*, August, 1906

Denver Post,
>May 25, 1949
>May 21, 1950
>September 23, 2009

Durango Herald, February 8, 2010

Fairplay Flume, January, 1882

Gulliford, Andrew, "The Donkey Devotion," *Durango Herald,* October 12, 2008

Harmon, Tracy, "So Looking for Burros, Eh?", *Pueblo Chieftain*, September, 2001

Herzog, Ralph, "The Evolution of Burro Racing," *Burro Days*, July 2009

Bibliography

Howe, Elvon L., editor, *Rocky Mountain Empire*, "Lady Jack-Whacker," Doubleday & Co., Garden City, New York, 1946

Imries, Curtis, "Year of the Donkey, A Collection of Ass-ays," 1997

Katz, Jon, "Nice Ass! Why I Own A Donkey," *Slate Magazine*, March 2, 2006

Kedro, M. James, "The Rocky Mountain Canary, An Unsung Hero," mindspring.com/-raleigh1/January 19, 2006

Kuhn, Tom, "Wild Burro Roundup," *Arizona Highways*, May 2, 2006

Layton, Lyndsey and Eilperin, Juliet, "Salazar Presents Ambitious Plan to Manage Wild Horses," *Washington Post*, October 8, 2009

Marcus, Richard, "Protected Wild Burros in Danger of Extinction," *Blog Critics Magazine*, February 19, 2008

Marshall, Julie Hoffman, "Donkeys Now Considered Intelligent and Loyal Pets," *Denver Post*, November 9, 2008

Miner, Carrie M., "Wild Burros Roam the Range Protecting Their Turf and Defending Their Young," *Arizona Highways*, July, 2000

The Miners World, (no author given), "The Burro's Service to Mining", Oct. 6, 1906 Volume XXV, No. 14, Pg. 427

"New Attention to Wild Horses," (no author given), *Santa Fe New Mexican*, January 24, 2010

New York Times, October, 2009

Noel, Tome, "A Day to Bray for Burros in Cripple Creek," *Rocky Mountain News*, June 23, 2001

Rocky Mountain Empire Magazine, *Denver Post*, April 30, 1950

Rocky Mountain News, July 21, 1949

Salazar, Ken, "At Home on the Range," *Los Angeles Times*, January 14, 2010

San Juan Prospector, March 28, 1873

Success Magazine, June, 1905

Walter, Hal, "Another Season on the Trail," *Colorado Central Magazine*, January, 2010

Walter, Hal, "Confessions of a Pack Burro Racer," *Colorado Central Magazine*, August, 2005

Walter, Hal, "The Future of Pack Burro Racing Will Come From Its Roots," *Colorado Central Magazine*, July, 2003

Wardell, William, "Memories of Aspen, Colorado," *The Colorado Magazine*, Colorado State Historical Society, Vol. XXXV, No. 2, April, 1958

"Wild Horse Advocates Aren't Doing the Animals Any Favors," *Reno Gazette Journal*, December 9, 2009

"Will Boom Days Bring Triple Crown Winner?" *Leadville Herald Democrat*, August 6, 2009

Films

"The Lost Frontier," produced by Curtis Imrie (a feature length film about pack burro racing and the West)

Pamphlets

"Adopt a Wild Horse or Burro," Bureau of Land Management, U. S. Department of the Interior, 2007

"Wild Horse and Burro National Program Office," Bureau of Land Management, U. S. Department of the Interior, no date

Index

ৡಖ

Index